# Endorse

The Clarks have made healing simple! That's the way God intended it.

In this fallen world, each one of us needs a healing of some kind, whether in our emotions, our beliefs, our relationships, or our body. Even for Christians who have studied the Bible for decades, the keys to God's healing power have often remained a mystery. Dennis and Dr. Jen Clark's groundbreaking book, *Releasing the Divine Healer Within,* provides both a theoretical framework and a step-by-step guide for believers on how to release the healing power of Christ within them. It does a masterful job in combining scriptural insights, modern science, and practical applications. Comparing biblical passages with the latest medical science, they present a compelling case that God wants to heal every area of your life—and much faster than you ever could have dreamed!

Dennis and Dr. Jen describe how our physical body, emotions, and spiritual being do not work in isolation but are integrated down to the cells and hormones. They have wonderful insight and are able to explain the science in thought-provoking ways.

*Releasing the Divine Healer Within* is a fascinating book, which is both easy to read and very powerful. The first chapter is intriguing, with amazing testimonies regarding organ transplants. That piqued my interest and had me wondering where this narrative would take me. The unexpected answer came later with instructions on how to strengthen your relationship with God as well as tap into the power of the Divine Healer. The principles are not only biblical, simple, and easy to understand, but they are also powerful, effective, and proven. This book would be of great benefit for new believers as well as mature saints. It only requires yielding to the Spirit of God. *"He will guide the humble in judgment and He will teach the humble His Way"* (Ps. 25:9 ONMB). I heartily recommend *Releasing the Divine Healer Within*.

WILLIAM J. MORFORD
Author/translator of the *One New Man Bible*

I love this book! It's not just another take on old truth but a fresh, new approach with far-reaching implications for divine health and healing. *Releasing the Divine Healer Within* teaches you how to experience Christ within your physical body, as well as thoughts, emotions, and choices—your entire person and personality. Dennis and Dr. Jen's ability to clearly explain biblical truths, correlate keys from medical science, and give practical tools for applying these truths will launch you into a truly healthy kingdom lifestyle, both inside and out.

PASTOR WESTON BROOKS
River of Life Christian Fellowship

# RELEASING
## THE
# DIVINE
# HEALER
### Within

## OTHER BOOKS BY
## DENNIS AND DR. JEN CLARK

*Live Free*

*Deep Relief Now*

*The Supernatural Power of Peace*

## OTHER EBOOKS BY
## DENNIS AND DR. JEN CLARK

*Simple Keys to Heal Rejection*

*Simple Keys to Heal Loneliness*

*Simple Keys for Self-Deliverance*

# RELEASING
## THE
# DIVINE
# HEALER
*Within*

*The Biology of Belief and Healing*

DENNIS *and* DR. JEN CLARK

*It's Supernatural* and Messianic Vision Inc.

4301 Westinghouse Blvd.

Charlotte, NC 28273

Cover and interior design by Terry Clifton

ISBN 13 TP: 978-0-7684-0748-8

ISBN 13 eBook: 978-0-7684-0749-5

For Worldwide Distribution, Printed in the U.S.A.

1 2 3 4 5 6 7 8 / 19 18 17 16 15

# DEDICATION

We dedicate *Releasing the Divine Healer Within* to our pastoral team—Jason Clark, our son and senior associate pastor; his wife, associate pastor Gwendolyn Clark; as well as associate pastors Cliff and Stina Coon, Vicky Rose, and Molly U. Tarr. Your unwavering support, encouragement, prayers, and commitment to the family mission mean more than we could possibly express.

We also dedicate this book to the believers, both children and adults, who put these principles into practice and are experiencing divine healing and miracles by yielding to the Divine Healer within their hearts. Your testimonies are truly an inspiration to us, and we pray that they will ignite faith for healing in multitudes of people around the world.

# ACKNOWLEDGMENTS

We are deeply grateful for all those who made this book possible, and wish to personally thank Destiny Image Publishers. It is always a great pleasure to work with you. For those who helped craft the first draft of the book, we are deeply grateful. We would also like to express our great appreciation to Rebecca Lebovich for proofreading, editing, and advising. You are a treasure!

# CONTENTS

# Chapter 1

# IDENTITY

Stories from organ transplant recipients illustrate the profound truth that our identity is written on every cell in our body. In *A Change of Heart*, Claire Sylvia, a conservative, health-conscious New England woman, tells the story of what she experienced after a heart and lung transplant. Following the surgery, she began to experience strange dreams and inexplicably developed a taste for beer, chicken nuggets, and motorcycles. This was completely out of character.

After a particularly vivid dream, Claire delved into the history of her organ donor and found out that he was an 18-year-old motorcycle enthusiast who loved chicken nuggets and beer. After much difficulty, she discovered his name was Tim L. and that he had died in a motorcycle accident. Along with her new heart cells apparently came a part of the young man—his memories—both his likes and dislikes.[1]

In *The Heart's Code*, psychologist Paul Pearsall describes the story of an eight-year-old girl who began to have nightmares following a heart transplant. The organ donor was another young girl, age ten. After the transplant, she began to have horrific dreams about a murder. They were so vivid and specific they eventually led to the capture of the murderer who had, in fact, killed the donor. Evidence from the nightmares included the time of the murder, the weapon, and the clothes the murderer wore. These details were all absolutely accurate.[2]

### Identity Is Written in Our Cells

These stories are just two among many hundreds of similar stories from organ transplant recipients who frequently experience memories and tastes of those whose organs they have received.[3] The impartation of inherited memories from organ donors into the personalities of recipients illustrates the profound truth that who we are is somehow written on our cells. How can this be?

"Identity" is not just the distinguishing personal conception, personality, or fingerprint signature of an individual. It is a biological reality down to the cellular level. Every cell in our body records our identity.[4] The surface of each one of our cells has "identity receptors" or *human leukocyte antigens* (HLA). Although our cells retain the same identity, the story told by our cells develops over the course of a lifetime. A chronicle of our entire life is continuously being recorded within our cells from cradle to grave. When we change, our cells change. Our biography becomes our biology. "We" are written in our cells!

Our unique "self" is encoded in our biological identity. Recognition of HLA by the immune system gives the cell its right to belong within a community of cells. The immune system won't accept cells with different identities, perceiving them to be foreign invaders.

---

*O*ur biography becomes our biology.

---

Of course this poses a problem in organ transplants. The identity receptors of the organ recipient will not recognize the "alien" identity of the transplanted organ . To prevent organ rejection, recipients of organ transplants must take medication that suppresses the activity of the immune system so their bodies won't try to destroy the transplanted organ.

### The Physical Environment Changes Cells

Our *nutritional* environment changes our cells. We all know that nutrition affects our health. Certain vitamins, for example, are recommended to strengthen our immune system. Many optometrists recommend vitamins for ocular health. Vitamins and supplements are good for joint health. Headlines regularly announce the discovery of new superfoods, dietary aids, or herbal supplements as the latest keys to good nutritional health. What we ingest makes a difference in our cells.

Physical environment plays a vital role in the health of cells. When a cell is ailing, check its environment. If an organism has too little water, the cells dehydrate. If it lacks essential nutrients, the cells become malnourished. If the cells of an organism are healthy, the organism is healthy and vice versa. Yet, is physical environment all there is to health?

### Emotions Change Cells

It is common knowledge that our *emotions* affect our physiology. Our face may turn red with embarrassment. Our voice can become shaky when we are nervous. Fear can make our hands tremble and our skin feel cold. Feelings of affection dilate the pupils of the eyes. Extreme anger may cause people to "see red." Rage redirects blood flow away from the frontal lobes of the brain, resulting in a decreased capacity for rational thought. (That is why a distinction is made in courts of law between crimes of passion and crimes that are premeditated.)

Scientific studies indicate that good and bad emotions,[5] our stress level,[6] and the quality of our social relationships[7] affect our entire body—down to the cellular level. (We will cover this more thoroughly in later chapters.) Many medical professionals regularly warn patients about stress in their lives because of its harmful effects on their bodies.

> Stress exists in your mind—but it's also evident in your stomach, heart, muscles and even your toes. "In fact, stress...[affects] every cell in your body," says Ronald Glaser, Ph.D., a researcher at [The] Ohio State University Medical School.[8]

Dr. Candace Pert, a neuroscientist who helped discover a fundamental element of brain chemistry in relation to emotions, made the amazing discovery that the *primary mechanism* of cellular change is emotional. Our *emotions* inscribe who we are on our cells. From the love of a mother during infancy to the emotional traumas of childhood to the worries of adulthood, everything is remembered by our cells. Emotional memory is stored at the cellular level.[9] The brain can think and remember, but who we truly are, our identity, is a matter of our emotional being. Our *emotions* inscribe who we are on our cells.

Molecules of emotion are the intercom system of the body. They inform all the cells about how we are responding to everything in life. How does this happen? Our emotions are transmitted throughout our entire body via tiny *signal hormones*. Our cells *read* emotional information through "emotion receptors" on the surface of each cell. Emotional information is received into our cells and identity receptors record the changes.

The identity receptors on our cells contain our entire life story. They tell what our life has been like. They record the beliefs of our innermost being. There is an old saying about people who don't hide their emotions: "Their heart is written on their sleeve." In truth, it would be more accurate to say, "Our heart is written on our cells."

*O*ur heart is written on our cells.

### The Holy Spirit Changes Cells

When we are born again, a spiritual transformation takes place. We become God-indwelt, a new creation! If a transplanted organ can change some aspects of an unbeliever's individual identity, how much more influence should our new creation identity have on us?

> *Therefore, if anyone is in Christ, he is a new creation; old things have passed away; behold, all things have become new (2 Corinthians 5:17).*

It is wonderful news for believers to know that we aren't bound by our past. Do you remember when you got saved?

Suddenly everything in life seemed new. Your thoughts changed, you made different choices, and your emotions were impacted. When you received forgiveness for your sins, you experienced peace with God for the first time. Although unbelievers can sometimes feel the peace of God in the atmosphere, Christians experience supernatural peace within. Because Jesus has given us His peace as a gift, it is always available for us (see John 14:27).

*O*ur *emotions* inscribe who we are on our cells.

Not everything in our lives is taken care of at the time of our conversion. We all have some pre-salvation baggage of unhealed emotional wounds and traumas. If we remember any situation and still feel pain (or any other negative emotion), it is still stored in cellular memory. The fact of an emotional wound is a matter of *historical record*. We can't change history.

When God heals us, however, we have a testimony—a new *heavenly record* of peace in our heart.[10] When the Holy Spirit cleanses our wounds and traumas, forgiveness *washes away* negative emotions. Toxic emotions in our cells are then *replaced* by the supernatural peace of God.

Our body, therefore, has the capacity to be changed in the presence of God. Moses made a bold and startling request of God in Exodus 33:18: *"Please, show me Your glory."* It is even more astonishing that God granted the desire of Moses's heart. What is God's glory—*kabod* in Hebrew? Glory is the sum total of all God is. His glory is the infinite splendor, majesty, beauty, and greatness of God in His manifold perfections. Glory is the brilliance of the presence of God.

> *T*oxic emotions in our cells can be *replaced* by the supernatural peace of God.

When God's presence manifests in fullness, we find His power, wisdom, holiness, justice, mercy, love, life, and radiant light—and every other attribute of His character and nature. Glory, then, is the shining forth of the essence of God. It is the very atmosphere of heaven itself. In response to the cry in the heart of Moses, God released the rays of His glory to Mount Sinai in the middle of a desert.

After 40 days and nights during which he was completely immersed in the glory cloud of God's presence, Moses came down the mountain and returned to the camp of the Israelites. The appearance of Moses was so different it was scary! His face was...glowing. The light was so bright everyone was frightened: *"When Aaron and all the children of Israel saw Moses, behold, the skin of his face shone, and they were afraid to come near him"* (Exod. 34:29-30). We can watch reality shows about extreme makeovers, but this was a makeover that tops them all.

Have you ever wondered *why* Moses's face shone after he came down from Mount Sinai? Being in the glory of God had actually transformed the cells of his body! How could this happen? We know that it was supernatural, but what physical mechanism in the human body could account for the visible change? Identity receptors.

When we are born again, we become a new creation spiritually, but the "new creation" *begins* to be imprinted on every cell. When our heart (our inner being) changes, our cells change. Who we become is imprinted on our cells. God created us with the physical capacity to be transformed in the very cells of our human body.[11] When we spend time in prayer and grow in grace and the knowledge of God, our cells reflect it.[12]

> *But we all, with unveiled face, beholding as in a mirror the glory of the Lord, are being transformed into the same image from glory to glory, just as by the Spirit of the Lord* (2 Corinthians 3:18).

Scientific research has documented the positive impact of prayer on human physiology.[13] Prayer is more than talking to God. Rather, prayer is being *with* God, spirit-to-Spirit. Every time we are in the presence of God, we are changed. *"The Lord...makes us more and more like him as we are changed into his glorious image"* (2 Cor. 3:18 NLT).

### *Cellular Symphony*

Scientific studies are regularly being published that further explain the physiology merging emotion, identity, and spirituality. This research contains some of the most compelling medical, social, and spiritual discoveries of the modern age. Some of the most amazing discoveries have demonstrated the powerful connection between emotions and the physical body.

Our body plays a *cellular symphony* that celebrates the very essence of our being.[14] When molecules of emotion encounter cell receptors, molecule and receptor vibrate and hum together, creating a cellular symphony that "sings" throughout our physical body.

[Molecules of emotion]...serve to weave the body's organs and systems into a single web that reacts to both internal and external environmental changes with complex, subtly orchestrated responses. [Molecules of emotion]...are the sheet music containing the notes, phrases, and rhythms that allow the orchestra—your body—to play as an integrated entity. And the music that results is the tone or feeling that you experience subjectively as your emotion.[15]

*O*ur cellular symphony resonates
with the love of God.

When we are in prayer, our *natural* emotions are infused with God's *supernatural love*. Our cellular symphony resonates with the love of God as He touches us with His presence. When the Bible says that believers *"sing a new song to the Lord,"* they really do (Ps. 96:1 NLT). Our whole new-creation being vibrates in harmony with God.

When the love of God touches our heart, our cells are flooded with *glory*. We may not experience the same *intensity* of glory that Moses experienced. However, Christ *in us* is our "confident expectation" of glory now, not just in the future (see Col. 1:27). In Jesus's prayer to His Father, He says, *"The glory which You gave Me I have given them"* (John 17:22). God is love, God is life, and God is light.

In the Bible, we also find many examples of light without the sun, but originating from a supernatural source. Most of these are associated with the glory of God, which in the Bible is usually manifested as light, although sometimes as fire. This is not surprising, as the Bible tells us that God is light (1 John 1:5; cf. John 8:12), and also that God is a consuming fire (Deuteronomy 4:24; Hebrews 12:29).[16]

As Moses discovered, we cannot spend time with God without being changed. God's glorious nature transforms us inside and out. *"For it is God who commanded light to shine out of darkness, who has shone in our hearts to give the light of the knowledge of the glory of God in the face of Jesus Christ"* (2 Cor. 4:6).

Have you ever seen the amazing displays of Christmas lights timed to music? It's a light orchestra. When God touches our heart, we become God's "light orchestra." He is the Conductor and we are the symphony. The more time we spend in the presence of the Lord, the more our cells reflect God's glorious light and resonate with His love!

*E*very time the love of God touches our heart, our cells are flooded with glory.

### ENDNOTES

1. C. Sylvia, *A Change of Heart,* (New York, NY: Grand Central Publishing, 2008), 5–10.

2. P. Pearsall, *The Heart's Code,* (New York, NY: Broadway Books, 1999), 7.

3. Among those who do report memory transfer, only a small portion of donor memory manifests.

4. B. Lipton, *The Biology of Belief: Unleashing the Power of Consciousness, Matter and Miracles,* (Santa Rosa, CA: Mountain of Love/Elite Books, 2005), 188–191.

5. C. Pert, *Molecules of Emotion: The Science behind Mind-Body Medicine,* (New York, NY, Scribner, 1997), 18-19.

6. E. Sternberg, *The Balance Within*, (New York, NY: W.H. Freeman and Company, 2001), 131.

7. J. Cacioppo and W. Patrick, *Loneliness: Human Nature and the Need for Social Connection*, (New York, NY: W.W. Norton and Company), 93–109; Sternberg, *The Balance Within*, 133–157.

8. D.A. Padgett and R. Glaser, "How Stress Influences the Immune Response," *Trends in Immunology* 24, no. 8 (2003): 444-448; K. Staywell, "Understanding the Stress/Health Connection," Rochester Institute of Technology. Retrieved July 8, 2013 from http://www.rit.edu/fa/betterme/sites/rit .edu.fa.betterme/files/docs/Understanding%20the %20Stress%20Health%20Connection.pdf.

9. Pert, *Molecules of Emotion,* 144–148.

10. The historical record reveals the sins of David, but repentance and forgiveness cleanse the heavenly, or spiritual, record. David committed adultery with Bathsheba and had her husband murdered (see 2 Sam. 11:1-17). However, God says of David, *"I have found David the son of Jesse, a man after My own heart, who will do all My will"* (Acts 13:22). In Psalm 51, a repentant David humbled himself before the Lord and received forgiveness: *"Purge me with hyssop, and I shall be*

*clean; wash me, and I shall be whiter than snow.... Create in me
a clean heart, O God"* (Ps. 51:7,10).

11.	There have been many eyewitness accounts of visible physical
manifestations due to inner spiritual experience throughout
history. The light that shone from John of St. Samson is just
one such example. "John of St. Samson...[1571–1636] was a
humble lay brother of the Carmelite Order.... It is said that
the spiritual light that flooded the lay brother's soul, and the
flames that consumed his interior, were revealed externally
by a certain radiance that was clearly visible." [J.C. Cruz,
*Mysteries, Marvels and Miracles: In the Lives of the Saints*,
(Charlotte, NC: TAN Press, 1970), 167.]

12.	"In these extraordinary states we often saw his face [John of
St. Samson] glowing and radiant with, I know not what kind
of luminous ray, which used to be reflected from it. I myself
witnessed it with a number of other trustworthy religious.
No one can doubt the truth of this since John himself wrote
in his Mystical Cabinet that he often experienced this light,
which spread from the center of his soul to all his faculties,
even to the exterior senses." [John of St. Samson, O. Carm.,
*Prayer, Aspiration and Contemplation*, trans. by Venard
Poslusney, O. Carm., (New York, NY: Alba House, 1975),
10.]

13.	R.B. Byrd, "Positive Therapeutic Effects of Intercessory Prayer
in a Coronary Care Unit Population," *Southern Medical
Journal* 81 (1988): 88-89; H.G. Koenig, et al., "Modeling
the Cross-sectional Relationships between Religion, Physical
Health, Social Support, and Depressive Symptoms," *American
Journal of Geriatric Psychiatry* 5 (1997), 131–144; H.G.
Koenig and A. Futterman, "Religion and Health Outcomes:
A Review and Synthesis of the Literature." Background paper,
published in proceedings of *Conference on Methodological
Approaches to the Study of Religion, Aging, and Health*,

sponsored by the National Institute on Aging, (March 16-17, 1995).

14.  Pert, *Molecules of Emotion,* 148.

15.  Ibid., 148.

16.  R. Grigg, "Light, Life and the Glory of God," *Creation Ministries International.* Retrieved November 18, 2014 from http://creation.com/light-life-and-the-glory-of-god.

*Chapter 2*

# A GLORIFIED BODY

The desire to find our true identity and destiny is a passion that burns in the heart of every individual born on earth. This yearning for identity and destiny is God-given—a seed of divine discontent planted in us by God at our birth.

At some point in life, we all ask, "Who am I?" and "Why am I here?"

> *T*he desire to find our true identity is a passion that burns in every heart.

### True Identity

The answer cannot be found in an education degree, job title, social status, unique talents, relationships, or even in good works. There is only one true answer to this question of identity. If you are a believer in the Lord Jesus Christ, your true identity is as a new creation (see 2 Cor. 5:17). Who you are *in Christ* is the real you. The new creation is who God created you to be from before the foundation of the world (see Eph. 1:4).

Father God carried you in His heart for eons of time in eternity past, and then, in the fullness of time, spoke you into existence to live for a short time here on earth (see Rom. 8:29). During your life journey on earth, the Holy Spirit is drawing you back to the heart of Father God (see Rom. 8:30; Eph. 1:5). Part of your mission during your time on this planet is to discover who you really are—not according to the world's standards and temporal measurements, but rather from an eternal perspective, as a born-again child of God.

*The* new-creation you is the real you.

How do we make this discovery?

When Jesus revealed to His disciples how to commune with God, He gave them the Lord's Prayer (see Matt. 6:9-13). This perfect prayer is like a "net" that begins with "Our Father," then reaches out to the limits of our fallen condition, drawing us back to an encounter with our Heavenly Father once again. Our spiritual progress is described in this prayer, starting with the end of the prayer. During our pilgrimage on earth, as we follow Jesus we are wooed back to our beginning and our real identity in Christ.

Let's look more closely at this "net" of the Lord's Prayer to understand our pilgrim's journey back to the Father, the source of our eternal identity. It begins when we recognize our need for a Savior. Consider this verse from John 6:44: Jesus said, *"No one can come to Me unless the Father who sent Me draws him."* The Greek word for "draw" is also translated "drag," which is the same verb used to describe how fishermen in Jesus's day would "drag" their nets ashore, filled with fish. Our Father literally "drags" us to His heart through His lovingkindness and grace.

This perfect prayer begins by telling us who our true Father is—God Himself. It ends with a description of His kingdom: *"power"* and *"glory forever"* (Matt. 6:13).

> *Our Father in heaven, hallowed be Your name. Your kingdom come. Your will be done on earth as it is in heaven. Give us this day our daily bread. And forgive us our debts, as we forgive our debtors. And do not lead us into temptation, but deliver us from the evil one. For Yours is the kingdom and the power and the glory forever* (Matthew 6:9-13).

The progression of our salvation begins with a Savior who can *"deliver us"* from evil (Matt. 6:13). Next, we find the peace of forgiving others because we ourselves have been forgiven (see Matt. 6:12). As we receive our daily portion of the bread of life in prayer, we become spiritually nourished (see Matt. 6:11). Through learning to love God's will, we desire that His kingdom come on earth through us. Like Jesus, we begin to say, *"I must be about my Father's business"* (Luke 2:49). Finally, we become mature sons and daughters unto the Father. We call God *our* Father, not just *the* Father!

With the recognition of our tremendous need for our Father and Creator, the One who holds the blueprint of our being, we begin our journey toward our true identity. In finding our Heavenly Father, we begin to discover ourselves!

*Our Father which art in heaven, hallowed be Thy name* (Matthew 6:9 KJV).

> $\mathscr{W}$e now call God *our* Father,
> not just *the* Father.

In the four Gospels, Jesus said, *"Follow Me"* a total of 17 times. This directive implies that He is *going somewhere,* and consequently, we are to follow Him. Where is He going, and where are we also to go? In the Book of John, Jesus says that He came from the Father and is returning to the Father. We are invited to follow Him back to Father's house: *"I shall prepare a place for you. I am coming again and I shall take you along with Me, so that where I AM you would also be"* (John 14:3 ONMB).

How is the new creation made *fully* manifest in us? In returning to the heart of the Father. As the fullness of Christ is revealed in and through us, we begin to know and experience our true identity as a new creation and discover our true destiny, found only in Christ. In returning to the Father, therefore, we discover both identity and destiny. The apostle Paul writes: *"We are God's [own] handiwork (His workmanship), recreated in Christ Jesus, [born anew] that we may do those good works which God predestined (planned beforehand)"* (Eph. 2:10 AMP).

In the Hebrew mindset, a son was mature when he was ready to run the family business alongside his father. In the

Song of Solomon, the Shulamite maiden begins her journey by running toward God but eventually becomes a colaborer with Him.

> *Come, my beloved, let us go forth to the field; let us lodge in the villages. Let us get up early to the vineyards; let us see if the vine has budded, whether the grape blossoms are open, and the pomegranates are in bloom. There I will give you my love* (Song of Solomon 7:11-12).

*In* returning to the Father, we discover both identity and destiny.

As we come to know Christ more intimately, His nature is engrafted into us. What results is what we really know of Him—what we have experienced in and through Him in our secret place of prayer and communion—can now be demonstrated to the world through us: *"As He is* [to us]*, so are we in this world"* (1 John 4:17 AMP).

Paul prays that believers will be *"filled [through all your being] unto all the fullness of God [may have the richest measure of the divine Presence, and become a body wholly filled and flooded with God Himself]!"* (Eph. 3:19 AMP). He also prays that this fullness will invade not our spirit alone, but that our *"spirit, soul, and body"* would all be wholly *sanctified*, or "set apart for God" (see 1 Thess. 5:23). "Sanctify" in the Greek is *hagiasmos*, meaning "separated unto God". Sanctification must be individually pursued, and we are being "built up, little by little as a result of obedience to the Word of God, of following the example of Christ...in the power of the Holy Spirit."[1]

---

*A*s He is to us, so are we in the world.

---

When Jesus died for us, He paid the price for wholeness in our spirit, soul, *and* physical body. The atonement clearly includes provision for healing and health (see Ps. 103:3; Isa. 53:5). This is not just so that we will feel better while we are on the earth, although God cares about every aspect of our lives. Rather, our physical bodies are very important to God and His eternal plans for the bride of Christ.

### *Jesus Received a Glorified Body*

Father God gave Jesus a physical body for a specific purpose—for the redemption of humanity—a body which was glorified after the Resurrection. When He ascended into heaven, Jesus ascended with a body. The Jesus who now sits at the right hand of Father God in heaven is not an incorporeal spirit. He is a Spirit being who has a glorified physical body for all eternity.

Prior to the Crucifixion, Jesus revealed a prophetic picture of His future glorified body on the Mount of Transfiguration. Matthew writes, *"He was transfigured before them. His face shone like the sun, and His clothes became as white as the light"* (Matt. 17:2). He displayed a measure of change—a glimpse of His glory.

After the Resurrection, Jesus received a glorified body. His physical body was changed in some fashion, yet still remained a physical "body." It was somehow the same, yet it was somehow different. This is why John writes after the fact:

*His disciples did not understand these things at first; but when Jesus was glorified, then they remembered that these things were written about Him and that they had done these things to Him* (John 12:16).

Mary Magdalene, a woman who had been well acquainted with Jesus in His earth walk, was the first witness of the Resurrection. When she saw Jesus in the garden, however, His appearance was so altered that she failed to recognize Him initially:

*Jesus said to her, "Woman, why are you weeping? Whom are you seeking?" She, supposing Him to be the gardener, said to Him, "Sir, if You have carried Him away, tell me where You have laid Him, and I will take Him away"* (John 20:15).

The two disciples on the road to Emmaus did not recognize the resurrected Jesus at first, even though they walked and talked with Him for seven miles.

*Now it came to pass, as He sat at the table with them, that He took bread, blessed and broke it, and gave it to them. Then their eyes were opened and they knew Him; and He vanished from their sight* (Luke 24:30-31).

We also find in Scripture that Jesus was not just a Spirit without a body. Although His body had the capacity to vanish and reappear, He could be physically touched—which is a very physical trait.

> *Jesus came, the doors being shut, and stood in the midst, and said, "Peace to you!" Then He said to Thomas, "Reach your finger here, and look at My hands; and reach your hand here, and put it into My side. Do not be unbelieving, but believing." And Thomas answered and said to Him, "My Lord and my God!"* (John 20:26-28)

However, even after the Resurrection, Jesus was not yet visible in His full glory. In Acts 1:9-12, we learn that the disciples watched our Lord Jesus ascend into the clouds and return to His Father. Later, however, He was revealed in the full radiance of His glory. When he was being stoned to death, Stephen looked heavenward and saw *"the glory of God, and Jesus standing at the right hand"* of Father God (Acts 7:55). In the Book of Revelation, the apostle John describes the glorified Jesus in heaven: His eyes were *"like a flame of fire"* and His face *"like the sun shining in its strength"* (Rev. 1:14,16).

### Believers Will Receive Glorified Bodies

If, in the natural, our heart determines who we are and that information is encoded in our physical body, what about our spiritual existence? Do we have a spiritual identity that transcends our earthly identity? And can that identity also be written in our cells? The Bible affirms that our new-creation identity will someday be manifested in our bodies as well as our spirit and soul: *"We shall be changed. For this corruptible must put on incorruption, and this mortal must put on immortality"* (1 Cor. 15:52-53).

We too will live in glorified bodies forever. Like Jesus, we will also be glorified. The Bible tells us that we *"will shine forth as the sun in the kingdom"* of our Father (Matt. 13:43). These glorified bodies in which we will live throughout eternity contain our identity just as our spirit contains our identity. Indeed, our bodies are so significant in God's plan for eternity future that we will also live in glorified bodies forever. Paul makes this abundantly clear throughout his writings:

> *If children, then heirs—heirs of God and joint heirs with Christ...that we may also be glorified together* (Romans 8:17).

> *L*ike Jesus, every believer will receive a glorified body.

Why should it surprise us that we can experience the glory in our bodies? Paintings of the early saints of Christianity showed them with halos representing the light radiating from their faces, just like Moses (see Exod. 34:29). Even today, it is not uncommon to see a supernatural glow on the face of a new believer or a person being touched by the Holy Spirit.

Someday we will be *fully* glorified. However, we don't have to wait until we go to heaven for our body to experience a measure of divine change. The Spirit of God can flood the cells of our physical body prior to the ultimate glorification of the body. We are not a product of earth, our past, or our genetics. We are who God says we are. We are spirit beings who came from God and are returning to our Father. We came from glory and are returning to glory.

God's ultimate purpose is for us to be fully transformed and to fully gain the heavenly life. We will still be "us" yet different. The apostle Paul wrote to the church at Corinth, reminding them of this very fact: *"Just as we have borne the image of the earthly man, so shall we bear the image of the heavenly man"* (1 Cor. 15:49 NIV).

*W*e are who God says we are.

### PRACTICE

#### WELCOME HEALING

- **Pray.** Close your eyes and put your hand on your heart (on your belly) and pray. Notice that when you close your eyes to pray, your focus shifts from your head to your heart.

- **Yield.** Yield, or open, your heart to the Divine Healer in you. Relax, don't try.

- **Welcome healing.** Welcome healing power into every cell of your body.

  Note: The Bible locates our spiritual heart in our belly (see John 7:38 KJV).

### ENDNOTE

1. W.E. Vine, *Vine's Expository Dictionary of Old and New Testament Words*, Vol. 4, (Old Tappan, NJ: Fleming H. Revell Company, 1981), 55-56.

*Chapter 3*

# THE BIOLOGY OF BELIEF

No major civilization has ever existed without some form of religion or concept of God. More than 90 percent of Americans believe there's a God.[1] Around the world, more than 80 percent of people identify with a religious group.[2] What is inside us, in the way we are made, that causes us to seek God?

We were created with needs that drive us to search for something to meet each need. We seek food when we are hungry. We seek water when we are thirsty. We seek a companion when we feel the need for relationship. We seek happiness because we sense our emptiness. As King Solomon lamented late in his life: *"I have seen all the works that are done under the sun; and indeed, all is vanity* [empty, meaningless] *and grasping for the wind"* (Eccl. 1:14).

As believers, we understand that the only way we can truly find satisfaction and contentment lies in discovering that which fills our greatest need—God Himself. Blaise Pascal

(1623–1662), French mathematician, physicist, inventor, and Christian philosopher, states:

> What...does this craving...proclaim but that there was once in man a true happiness, of which all that now remains is the empty print and trace? This he tries in vain to fill with everything around him, seeking in things that are not there the help he cannot find in those that are, though none can help, since this infinite abyss can be filled only with an infinite and immutable object; in other words by God himself.[3]

### Born to Believe

We are born to believe. We seek God because we were *created* to need Him. Furthermore, the Lord made us with the capacity to *find* Him. *"You will seek Me and find Me, when you search for Me with all your heart. I will be found by you"* (Jer. 29:13-14). And: *"When You said, 'Seek My face,' my heart said to You, 'Your face, Lord, I will seek'"* (Ps. 27:8). As it turns out, science supports what the Bible has said all along.

Dr. Andrew Newberg, medical doctor and neuroscientist, has researched the relationship between brain function and various mental states and has pioneered a field of research called *neurotheology*, which studies how the brain responds to and perceives religious and spiritual experiences. He hypothesizes that human beings throughout the ages have sought God because He has equipped us with "transcendent machinery" so we can discover Him.[4] It appears that God created us with the *ability* to believe in Him and make a connection with Him.

*G*od has equipped us
so we can discover Him.

### Emotions and Spiritual Experience

The emotional center of the brain, the limbic system, is very active in spiritual experience. Just as we can't define spirituality without cognitive understanding, it appears that the emotions are essential in religion and spirituality. In other words, both head and heart function together as one in all religious perceptions. Scientists studying the neuroscience of spiritual experience have found that all genuine spiritual experience profoundly impacts the emotions.

> The human limbic system [the emotional center of the brain] interweaves emotional impulses with higher thoughts and perceptions to produce a broad, flexible repertoire of complex emotional states.... Studies have also indicated that the limbic system is integral to religious and spiritual experiences.... Because of its involvement in religious and spiritual experiences, the limbic system has sometimes been referred to as the "transmitter to God."[5]

### Emotional Value Operator

The brain has seven cognitive operators that allow us to interpret the world around us as mental perceptions.[6] They control how sensory, thought, or memory inputs are related to each other and are translated into adaptive behaviors, thoughts, and emotions. However, the driving force behind our survival as a species is our emotional evaluation. According to the somatic marker hypothesis as proposed by Dr. Antonio Damasio in his book *The Feeling of What Happens*, "emotion is integral to the processes of reasoning and decision making."[7] The emotions provide the necessary "push" that drives and directs our behavior.

The emotional value operator "exists to assign an emotional valence to all the elements of perception and cognition.... Without the emotional value function, we would move through the world like very intelligent robots.... By investing...important behaviors with emotional value, the brain ensures that we will pursue survival intensely and passionately."[8]

The emotional value operator assigns levels of emotional importance to sensory input, thoughts, and perceptions by connecting the limbic system and the other cognitive operators. It allows us to know how we feel about something. This operator is crucial in determining the emotional responses individuals have during spiritual experiences.

Apparently, we are *emotionally programmed* to search for God.

### Neuroscience and Spiritual Experience

It appears that four association areas in the brain are keys in the mystical potential of the mind. These include the visual, verbal-conceptual, attention, and orientation association areas.

These four association areas are the most complex neurological structures in the brain. Their rich, fully integrated perceptions allow us to experience reality as a vivid, cohesive whole that flows smoothly and comprehensibly from one moment to the next.[9]

During times of intense prayer, brain scans reveal that the three association areas listed below show heightened neurological activity. Those centers are responsible for processing visual imagery, abstract concepts, and focused attention. Therefore, we would expect these results when studying spirituality and brain activity.

### The Visual Association Area (VAA)

The VAA is believed to play a "prominent role in religious and spiritual experiences that involve visual imagery." Newberg states that "spontaneous visions" in prayer or reported experiences "associated with unusual spiritual states such as near-death experiences may...originate in this area."[10]

### The Verbal-Conceptual Association Area (VCAA)

The verbal-conceptual association area is the junction of the temporal, parietal, and occipital lobes and is responsible for forming abstract concepts and verbally describing them. It is important for all mental functioning and is "important in religious experience, since almost all religious experiences have a cognitive or conceptual component—that is, some part that we can think about and understand."[11]

### The Attention Association Area (AAA)

Also known as the prefrontal cortex, the attention association area (AAA) has a significant role in the oversight of complex movements and behaviors related to attaining goals. "This structure is so heavily involved in such intentional behavior, in fact, that a number of researchers think of the attention area as the neurological seat of the will."[12]

In other words, it may be the area of the brain that intersects with our emotions to impel us to action. "We believe that part of the reason the attention association area is activated during spiritual practices [such as prayer]...is because it is heavily involved in emotional responses—and religious experiences are usually highly emotional."[13]

### God Increases as Self Decreases

The big surprise was the discovery that the orientation association area showed *decreased* activity in brain scans. A key area in the brain that defines "self" (the orientation association area, or OAA) shows significantly diminished brain activity during intense prayer.

> We know that the orientation area never rests, so what could account for this unusual drop in activity levels in this small section of the brain? As we pondered the question, a fascinating possibility emerged. What if the orientation area was working as hard as ever, but the incoming flow of sensory information had somehow been blocked? That would explain the drop in brain activity in the region. More compellingly, it would also mean that the OAA had been temporarily "blinded," deprived of the information it needed to do its job properly.[14]

When we pray, *self* decreases and *God* increases (see John 3:30). Consider the words of 13th-century Franciscan sister Angela of Foligno: "How great is the mercy of the one who realized this union.... I possessed God so fully that I was no longer in my previous customary state but was led to find a peace in which I was united with God and was content with everything."[15]

At such times, our spirit overrides our normal self-awareness somehow, allowing us to encounter a spiritual realm that proves its own reality. Teresa of Avila reports, "God visits the soul in a way that prevents it doubting when it comes to itself that it has been in God and God in it...and so firmly is it convinced of this truth that, though years may pass before this state recurs, the soul can never forget it, to doubt its reality."[16]

> The mind remembers mystical experience with the same degree of clarity and sense of reality that it bestows upon memories of "real" past events. The same cannot be said of hallucinations, delusions, or dreams. We believe this sense of realness strongly suggests that the accounts of the mystics are not indications of minds in disarray, but are the proper, predictable neurological result of a stable, coherent mind willing itself to a higher spiritual plane.[17]

Science has now verified that we are made with the "equipment" to seek God and find Him.[18] It appears that our brain has transcendent machinery that joins head and heart together in spiritual experience.[19] "Science has surprised us, and our research has left us no choice but to conclude...that the mind's machinery of transcendence may in fact be a window through which we can glimpse the ultimate realness of something that is truly divine."[20] As a result of his research, Dr. Newberg has reached the conclusion that our encounters with God are biologically, observably, and measurably real. If we are created to discover God, and we are, then our experience of Him is limited only by the diligence of our pursuit.

> *O*ur experience of God is limited only
> by the diligence of our pursuit.

### Faith and Conscious Focus

How do we discover more of God and receive spiritual blessings from Him? We must believe and receive. Belief is a cognitive agreement in conjunction with a persuasion of heart. Faith is not just a "leap in the dark" or taking someone's word for something without evidence. An oft-quoted Scripture about faith is Hebrews 11:1: *"Faith is the substance of things hoped for, the evidence of things not seen."*

The word "substance" used in this verse is *hupostasis* in the Greek. "It speaks of the Divine essence of God" giving us a confident assurance in our heart.[21] Substance is not "nothing." Rather, it is a tangible *knowing*. When we hear a believer saying, "I know that I know I am saved," they are referring to spiritual *substance*. They reference two ways of knowing—knowledge in their head and assurance in their heart.

> *F*aith is the ability to believe God
> with the assurance in our heart.

Faith, then, is *the ability to believe God with assurance in our heart*. With increased faith, *we believe God more* and, consequently, receive more from Him.

Our heart determines what we believe and receive. Consider the words of Jesus to the Pharisees: *"These people draw near to Me with their mouth, and honor Me with their lips, but their heart is far from Me"* (Matt. 15:7-8). Jesus chastised them because their hearts didn't believe what their mouths were speaking.

### Location

The first key to receiving is found in *location*. We must know *where* to receive. We must receive in our heart, not just our head. If we know something in our head but haven't received it in our heart, it is not yet real to us. Both *head and heart* must cooperate in believing.

> *B*oth head and heart must
> cooperate in believing.

The second key to receiving is *belief*. Jesus tells us: *"If you can believe, all things are possible to him who believes"* (Mark 9:23). And: *"Whatever things you ask when you pray, believe that you receive them, and you will have them"* (Mark 11:24).

Many believers believe erroneously that the word *heart* in the Bible refers to the physical heart in the chest, especially because so many modern translations have substituted the generic word *heart* for the original Hebrew and Greek words. When the Bible talks about the heart of man, it refers to the "belly" or "bowels" (the actual words used in both the Hebrew Old Testament and the Greek New Testament). This doesn't mean your heart and spirit are in a physical organ of the body. It just means the belly is the epicenter of spiritual and emotional activity.

In the Old Testament, the word *bowels* is used in older translations such as the King James Version of the Bible, but *heart* is used in later translations. When the Shulamite's Beloved came to her, she says, *"My bowels were moved for him,"* meaning that her heart was moved with affection (Song of Sol. 5:4 KJV). The Hebrew word here is *me'ah*, meaning "inward parts, digestive organs, bowels, womb, or, figuratively, the place of emotions of distress or love."

In the New Testament, the heart of man is also located in the belly. Jesus said, *"He that believeth on me, as the scripture hath said, out of his belly shall flow rivers of living water,"* indicating that the epicenter of spiritual activity is in the belly area (John 7:38 KJV). In the original Greek, the word used here is *koilia*, meaning *belly*. Later translations use the English word *heart* instead of belly, but belly is the more accurate translation.

> *The epicenter of spiritual activity is in the belly.*

Only one verse in the New Testament refers to the physical heart, Luke 21:26: *"men's hearts failing them from fear"* (KJV). With this one exception, the word *heart, kardia* in Greek, always refers to the innermost being. According to *Vine's Expository Dictionary of Old and New Testament Words*:

> By easy transition the word came to stand for man's entire mental and moral activity, both the rational and emotional elements. In other words, the heart is used figuratively for the hidden springs of the personal life.... Scripture regards the heart as the sphere of Divine influence.[22]

What happens when the Holy Spirit rules our heart and takes ascendancy over our thoughts, feelings, and will? *Revelation* rules our thoughts, *conscience* rules our will, and *communion* or *fellowship* with Christ rules our emotions.

*T*he heart is the sphere of Divine influence.

### "Bucket Man"

The location of our *conscious focus* is also a key to faith. Of course our thoughts are in our head, but our will and emotions are not as easy to locate. The will and emotions are not found in the physical organ of our heart. Rather, the Scriptures explain that our will and emotions are located in the *inner man*. The location of this *inner man* is found in the navel area, not the chest cavity (see John 7:38 KJV).

The Holy Spirit must rule in the heart, in the *inner man,* which is located in the belly area. Our spirit fills us from head to toe, but the epicenter of spiritual activity is in the belly. That is where we need to focus our conscious attention.

When Dennis was teaching me (Jen) how to drop down to my spirit, he used the analogy of dropping a bucket down a well. Focus is like a spiritual "bucket" inside. When we focus, we "pay attention." He told me that, when we focus on Messiah in our heart, we drop our bucket down to our spirit. However, when we focus on our own thoughts, we pull the bucket back up to our head.

To teach the children in Sunday school this concept, I made a "bucket man" poster as a visual aid. Over bucket man's head, there's a picture of a crank with rope wrapped around it with a hole in the middle. A piece of string goes through the hole and is tied to a cardboard bucket to pull it up and down. When the bucket goes down, we velcro a piece of blue cardboard water to the bucket to represent living water, but, when the bucket is drawn back up to bucket man's head, we remove the water.

When teaching some children at a Christian elementary school the principle of dropping down to our spirit, one commented, "Of course we have to drop down to our heart. We don't have living water in our head!

When the door of our heart opens to include God, our bucket goes down to the fountain of living water in our heart. When we focus on our head, the door of our heart closes and our bucket goes up. When we focus on our own thoughts apart from God, our bucket goes up where there is no living water influencing our thoughts. The children love the bucket man illustration, but we occasionally borrow him to teach adults as well.

> *Counsel in the heart of man is like water in a deep well, but a man of understanding draws it out* (Proverbs 20:5 AMP).

> *Whoever drinks of the water that I shall give him will never thirst. But the water that I shall give him will become in him a fountain of water springing up into everlasting life* (John 4:14).

If you ever sat quietly in church with an attitude of reverence toward God, whether or not you were aware of it, you most likely "dropped down" to your spirit. You may know intellectually that God is omnipresent, but when you focus on the fact that He is always with you, even at this very moment, your perception shifts based on this awareness. He is not only our Savior but our Immanuel, or *"God with us"* (see Matt. 1:23).

> *I will never leave you nor forsake you* (Hebrews 13:5).

> *God is our refuge and strength, a very present help in trouble* (Psalm 46:1).

When we open our heart to include the Lord, the peace we feel is a gentle sense that Someone else is with us. It is much the same as driving a car with a passenger in the back seat. You may not be able to see them, but you know they are there. When Dennis was teaching me about peace and the presence of God, he reminded me to "include God" in the moment. For example, when I became anxious about something, he would tell me,

"Open your heart to God and include Him." I quickly learned that whenever I became troubled, I was actually cutting God out of the picture and relying on my own efforts. As soon as I acknowledged God again and welcomed His help, I felt calm. The more I practiced, the more consistent I became at including the Lord in everyday life.

As soon as I opened my heart to God, I could feel a gentle sense of calmness and my perception of the world around me changed in a subtle but tangible way. It felt like an assurance that the Lord was with me but it wasn't lightning bolts or euphoria. Peace is often so faint it could also be described as "quiet stillness" or a feeling of relaxation. At any rate, no matter how we describe it, the peace of God's presence is the opposite of anxiety.

Proverbs 3:5-6 tells us, *"Trust in the Lord with all your heart, and lean not on your own understanding; in all your ways acknowledge Him, and He shall direct your paths."* Notice that we are instructed to trust in the Lord in our *heart* rather than relying upon our mental reasoning. The word *acknowledge* is *yâda* in Hebrew, meaning "to know" in a relational sense. It is often used for intimate union between husband and wife (see Gen. 4:1,17,25). As used here, *yâda* refers to divine intimate connection with the Lord. We make a heart connection with *Messiah in us* when we drop our bucket down to our heart.

### Troubleshooting

Quite often, people who say they can't feel peace have an unrealistic expectation. Everyone knows the difference between feeling relaxed and being upset, even a nonbeliever. As believers, however, relaxing allows *supernatural peace* to take the ascendancy and rule in our life in obedience to Scripture. Jesus has given us the gift of peace (see John 14:27). Peace should be the *starting place* for living the Christian life. The Scriptures command us to *"let the peace of God rule"* in our life (Col. 3:15).

It is interesting to note that children never seem to have a problem feeling the peace of God's presence, although they sometimes use the word *good* instead of *peace*. Adults have difficulty when they have made a habitual practice of "compartmentalizing," living out of their head rather than their heart.

Our expectations and practiced way of life can make living in peace harder than it should be. Most supernatural peace is too quiet for our flesh. We must *learn* to be still.

Psalm 46:10 commands us: *"Be still and know that I am God."* "Be still" comes from the Hiphil stem of the verb *rapha,* meaning "let go, surrender, or release." This verse contains two imperatives. We are to first *be still* and then *know* the power of God in our life. We are not to ponder the words but experience the mediation of the kingdom of God in our heart. As we surrender our control to God's control, we can experience His all-sufficiency. In doing so, we are delivered from our fears and find supernatural peace.

> *Surely I have calmed and quieted my soul, like a weaned child with his mother; like a weaned child is my soul within me* (Psalm 131:2).

Although some individuals may instantly feel the presence of God strongly when they drop down to their spirit, over time the sense of His presence will increase for all. The absence of turmoil is a good starting point, but your awareness of God's presence will grow when you continue the practice of yielding to Messiah within.

## PRACTICE

Sit down in a quiet room and close your eyes. Place your hand on your belly. Relax and yield to Messiah in you. Focus on your heart but notice that the atmosphere of the room also feels more peaceful. You become more aware of the Lord when you pay attention to Him.

Honor God by acknowledging the fact that He is with you. The Lord is not only omnipresent, but you are also God indwelt. When you invite Him into your heart, He never leaves you.

Spend a few minutes waiting in the presence of God. Often, as we become more relaxed, our awareness of peace increases.

We shouldn't ever attempt to make our mind go blank, but simply become aware that the Lord is with us by paying attention to Him. Focus is the opposite of "blank."

### The Biology of Belief

We are made with the capacity to believe, and what our heart believes is written in our cells. We cannot separate our beliefs from our physiology. What we believe in our heart touches every cell, organ, and system in our body. "Cells possess a uniquely 'tuned' receptor protein for every environmental signal that needs to be read."[23] In addition to identity receptors, our cells have "energy" receptors that respond to what we know as *spirit*. What we believe in our heart is *communicated* to our cells by emotions and the "energy" released through our faith. Faith is a *spiritual* connection with God's *spiritual* kingdom.

Cell *receptors* embedded in the cell membrane are a special class of proteins called Integral Membrane Proteins (IMPs). They open and close based on the signals they *receive*. Certain receptors respond to the physical environment, as mentioned previously. However, other receptors respond only to what scientists call "energy," including *spiritual* energy. The idea that only physical molecules can influence cell physiology has been proven wrong. Biological behavior can also be controlled by energy fields.[24]

What we believe in our heart is released through faith and communicated to our cells. Believing for healing is not merely asking God to *give* us something in prayer; it is *receiving healing anointing*. We can receive healing power from the prayers of others or directly from the Divine Healer in our own heart. Regardless of the means, God created us with the capacity to *yield* to healing, not just pray *for* healing. When we open our heart to the Healer, our cells open their gates to receive Him as well.

> *What* we believe in our heart is released
> through faith and communicated to our cells.

### Belief and Health

We have all heard of the "placebo effect," in which patients taking "sugar pills" in medical trials improve when they *believe* they are taking real medication. The American Medical Association defines a *placebo* as a "substance provided to a patient that the physician believes has no specific pharmacological effect upon the condition being treated." In medical research, placebos are given as a control treatment to some subjects while other patients are given an active drug. In these trials, the subjects don't know if they are taking the actual medication or a placebo.

The placebo effect has been considered an annoying artifact in clinical trials. However, the therapeutic effect of placebos is not just an artifact; it is a demonstration of the power of belief. As it turns out, what we believe in our heart is a powerful "medicine," even if the treatment itself is faulty. We can believe in sugar pills, bogus remedies, or a wrong diagnosis. Belief is what counts!

> A man whom his doctors referred to as "Mr. Wright" was dying from cancer of the lymph nodes. Orange-sized tumors had invaded his neck, groin, chest and abdomen, and his doctors had exhausted all available treatments. Nevertheless, Mr. Wright was confident that a new anticancer drug called Krebiozen would cure him, according to a 1957 report by psychologist Bruno Klopfer of the University of California, Los Angeles, entitled "Psychological Variables in Human Cancer."

> Mr. Wright was bedridden and fighting for each breath when he received his first injection. But three days later he was cheerfully ambling around the unit, joking with the nurses. Mr. Wright's tumors had shrunk by half, and after 10 more days of treatment he was discharged from the hospital. And yet the other patients in the hospital who had received Krebiozen showed no improvement.[25]

### The Power of Negative Beliefs

A negative belief can have a *negative effect* as demonstrated by the "nocebo effect." In 1974, Sam Londe was informed by his physician that he had cancer of the esophagus, which was considered to be 100 percent fatal at that time. Several weeks after his diagnosis, Londe passed away.

> The surprise came after Londe's death when an autopsy found very little cancer in his body, certainly not enough to kill him. There were a couple of spots in the liver and one in the lung, but there was no trace of the esophageal cancer that everyone thought had killed him.... [His doctor, Sam Meador, later said] "I thought he had [terminal] cancer. He thought he had [terminal] cancer.... Did I remove hope in some way?"[26]

What could explain these findings? Our thoughts and *heart* are connected. Although we may fool others or try to fool ourselves, our innermost being continuously whispers what we *believe* in our heart.

---

*O*ur innermost being continuously whispers what we *believe* in our heart.

---

In other words, if we believe we can or we believe we can't, we are right. Belief itself is the key. To reiterate: positive thinking alone has no power. Belief *must* include our heart. We can *make the choice* for life by believing the Lord and dealing with any barriers that prevent us from receiving the promises of God. This is why God says in His Word: *"I*

*have set before you life and death, blessing and cursing; there-*
*fore choose life"* (Deut. 30:19).

The healing power of the Divine Healer is in our own
heart: *"All things are possible to him who believes"* (Mark 9:23).
We make the connection with Him through our belief.

> *"All* things are possible
> to him who believes!"

## PRACTICE
### PRAY: Prayer Step 1

Notice that when you close your eyes to pray, your focus shifts from your head to your spiritual heart in your belly (see John 7:38 KJV). Yield to Christ within.

*PRACTICE: Pray*

Prayer is fellowship with a Person. Come into the presence of the Divine Healer to honor Him.

- *Pray.* Close your eyes and pray, placing your hand on your belly.
- *Focus.* Focus on Christ within.
- *Feel peace.* Yield and feel peace.

### RECEIVE: Prayer Step 2

*PRACTICE: Receive*

- *Pray.* Close your eyes and pray, placing your hand on your belly.
- *Yield.* Yield to the Divine Healer in your heart.
- *Receive.* Welcome healing into every cell of your body.

## TROUBLESHOOTING
### Removing Fear

- *Pray.* Close your eyes and pray, placing your hand on your belly.
- *First.* You may see a situation, another person, or yourself.
- *Feel.* Allow yourself to feel the fear momentarily.
- *Forgive.* Receive forgiveness for taking in fear (see 1 John 4:18).

# ENDNOTES

1.  "More than 9 in 10 Americans continue to believe in God," *Gallup Poll* (June 3, 2011). Retrieved September 8, 2013 from http://www.gallup.com/poll/147887/Americans-Continue-Believe-God.aspx.

2.  "The global religious landscape," *Pew Research Center*, Religion and Public Life (December 18, 2012). Retrieved September 8, 2013 from http://www.pewforum.org/2012/12/18/global-religious-landscape-exec/.

3.  B. Pascal, *Les Pensées*, (New York, NY: Penguin Books, 1966), 75.

4.  A. Newberg, E. d'Aquili, and V. Rause, *Why God Won't Go Away: Brain Science and the Biology of Belief,* (New York, NY: Ballantine Books, Random House Publishing Group, 2001), 8, 140-141.

5.  Ibid., 42-43.

6.  Seven cognitive operators have been identified: Holistic Operator, Reductionistic Operator, Causal Operator, Abstractive Operator, Binary Operator, Quantitative Operator, and the Emotional Value Operator.

7.  A. Damasio, *The Feeling of What Happens: Body and Emotion in the Making of Consciousness,* (Orlando, FL: Harcourt, Inc., 1999), 41.

8.  Newberg, *Why God Won't Go Away*, 52-53.

9.  Ibid., 32.

10. Ibid., 27.

11. Ibid., 31; E.R. Kandel, J.H. Schwartz, and T.M. Jessell, *Principles of Neural Science*, (New York, NY: McGraw Hill, 2000).

12. Newberg, *Why God Won't Go Away*, 29; C.D. Frith, P.F. Liddle, and R.S.J. Frackowiak, "Willed Action and the

Prefrontal Cortex in Man," *Proceedings of the Royal Society of London* 244 (1991), 241–246; R. Joseph, "The right cerebral hemisphere: emotion, music, visual-spatial skills, body image, dreams, and awareness," *Journal of Clinical Psychology* 44 (1988). 630–673; R. Joseph, *The Transmitter to God: the Limbic System, the Soul, and Spirituality,* (San Jose, CA: University Press California, 2000); B. Libet, A. Freeman, and K. Sutherland, *The Volitional Brain: Toward a Neuroscience of Free Will,* (Thorverton, UK: Imprint Academic, 1999).

13. Newberg, *Why God Won't Go Away*, 31.

14. Ibid. 4-6.

15. A. Foligno, *Complete Works,* (Mahwah, NJ: Paulist Press, 1993), 214–216.

16. T. and B. Zimmerman, *The Interior Castle: Or, The Mansions* (London: Thomas Baker, 1946), 79.

17. Newberg, *Why God Won't Go Away*, 6-7, 113, 174.

18. Ibid., 113, 174.

19. Humans are spirit beings who have souls (thoughts, will, and emotions) and live in bodies. (Animals consist of only soul and body.) God has given us the capacity to interact with the realm of the Spirit and discover Him. When we are born again, our spirit is made alive unto God and can then touch God's Spirit. Unsaved individuals also have spirits, but their spirits are "dead," or separated from God.

Both believer and nonbeliever can have spiritual experiences. The question is, what spiritual realm is contacted—evil or Holy? For those seeking deep spiritual experience, or "transcendent states," there is a primary difference between *how* they seek and *what* they seek. Scientists have studied both Christians and non-Christians, people of all types of religious persuasions, and found the neural evidence of spiritual experience is very similar (when studied on brain scans). It should not be surprising that our spiritual capacity can be used both for good and evil. However, when we come to God, we come in faith believing that we can safely open our heart to Him.

> *If a son asks for bread from any father among you, will he give him a stone? Or if he asks for a fish, will he give him a serpent instead of a fish? Or if he asks for an egg, will he offer him a scorpion? If you then, being evil, know how to give good gifts to your children, how much more will your heavenly Father give the Holy Spirit to those who ask Him!* (Luke 11:11-13)

The Christian approach is an active seeking with the intention to quiet the soul (carnal mind, will, and emotions), transcend self, and focus intently on a personal God. Thoughts, emotions, and perceptions are brought under the control of the Holy Spirit and yielded to the Lord. The goal is drawing closer to God. Self is not obliterated but cedes authority to God.

Practitioners of other religions, including new age and eastern mysticism, seek a state of pure awareness, or consciousness of "everything" as an undifferentiated whole through passive seeking. They attempt to clear, or blank out, thoughts, emotions, and perceptions to merge with "everything" and obliterate self. They do not seek a deity who is "out there" and separate from humankind. They believe that the entire universe is part of a cosmic consciousness, or force, with which everything can merge, and become "no-thing," much like pureed vegetable soup.

20.  Newberg, *Why God Won't Go Away*, 140-141.

21. W.E. Vine, *Vine's Expository Dictionary of Old and New Testament Words*, Vol. 2, (Old Tappan, NJ: Fleming H. Revell Company, 1981), 88.

22. Ibid., 206-207.

23. Lipton, *The Biology of Belief*, 83.

24. Ibid., 84, 99.

25. B. Klopfer, "Psychological Variables in Human Cancer," *Journal of Projective Techniques*, Vol. 21, no. 4, (December 1957), 331–340; M. Niemi, "Placebo Effect: A Cure in the Mind," *Scientific American*, (February/March 2009). Retrieved April 3, 2010 from http://www.scientificamerican.com/article/placebo-effect-a-cure-in-the-mind/.

26. Discovery, "Placebo: Mind over Medicine?" *Medical Mysteries*, (Silver Springs, MD, 2003), Discovery Health Channel; Lipton, *The Biology of Belief*, 142-143.

*Chapter 4*

# THE GOD WHO HEALS

The word *name* had a far greater significance for the children of Israel than what we understand today. For us, personal names serve mostly as labels to identify who is who. In ancient Israel, however, the "name" referred to the character, nature, and calling of a person. The names of God in Scripture are the names God calls Himself. Each one provides additional revelation about His character, work, ways, and relationship to us.

### The Names of God

The name *Jehovah* identifies God as the independent, self-existent God who gives revelation and provides redemption. It is used in the Scriptures almost 7,000 times. The Bible also contains various compound names of Jehovah, each of which signifies an important and distinct aspect of His redemptive nature. Whatever our need may be, God will be there for us in that facet of His character and nature.

> *A* name refers to the character,
> nature, and calling of a person.

Do we have an unmet need? God is *Jehovah-Jireh*, "the Lord my Provider" (see Gen. 22:14). Are we afraid? God is *Jehovah-Shalom*, "the Lord is my Peace" (see Judg. 6:23-24). Do we feel alone? We can count on God being with us as *Jehovah-Shammah*, "the Lord there" (see Ezek. 48:35).

When God first revealed Himself to Moses at the burning bush, He called Himself "I AM." This name is related to "Jehovah," and both names are derived from the Hebrew verb "to be."

> *Then Moses said to God, "Indeed, when I come to the children of Israel and say to them, 'The God of your fathers has sent me to you,' and they say to me, 'What is His name?' what shall I say to them?" And God said to Moses, "I AM WHO I AM." And He said, "Thus you shall say to the children of Israel, 'I AM has sent me to you.'" Moreover God said to Moses, "Thus you shall say to the children of Israel: 'The Lord God of your fathers, the God of Abraham, the God of Isaac, and the God of Jacob, has sent me to you. This is My name forever, and this is My memorial to all generations'"* (Exodus 3:13-15).

In Hebrew, "I AM" is composed of the words *ehyeh asher ehyeh*, literally meaning "I will be what I will be" or "I shall prove to be whatsoever I shall prove to be." What "I AM" do you need? God will be that "I AM" for you today, in whatever situation you may find yourself.

## *What* "I AM" do you need?

God miraculously delivered the children of Israel out of slavery in Egypt, parted the waters of the Red Sea providing a way of escape from the Egyptians pursuing them, and drowned Pharaoh and his armies in that same sea. However, a good and merciful God had a trial planned for the children of Israel.

Why would a loving God allow tribulation in the lives of His people? God reveals His power and mercy the most in times of hardship. How could the Lord prove Himself strong on our behalf if our life had no trials? God shows us He is with us in the difficulties of life as well as in the times of ease and comfort. Scripture tells us that God "works all things together for good" when we are in His will (see Rom. 8:28).

God led the Israelites into the wilderness of Shur, where they wandered three days without water. The blazing sun must have scorched them from above while they trudged through burning hot sand. Doubtless, their children cried out with parched tongues, and their cattle lowed in distress.

When the children of Israel finally saw the waters of Marah, how they must have rejoiced. But, alas! Their hope and anticipation quickly turned into despair when they tasted the bitter, undrinkable water. They became angry with Moses and complained against him. How quickly they had forgotten the goodness and power of God that had been demonstrated in their deliverance from Egypt and the miraculous parting of the Red Sea (see Exod. 15:23-24).

Moses cried out to the Lord on their behalf, and God showed him a tree, directing Moses to throw it into the water (see Exod. 15:25). Instantly the waters were healed and they could quench their thirst at last. God led the children of Israel to Marah to teach them more about Himself, the source of living waters and the God who heals.

*G*od uses trials to teach us about Himself.

This is the first reference to healing in the Bible. Moses believed God and threw an ordinary tree into the waters of Marah. Responding to this act of faith, God healed the bitter waters and made them drinkable. The same God who healed bitter waters also heals our body and soul.[1]

The Lord revealed Himself as the Healer of His people, *Jehovah-Rapha*, and promised them, *"If you diligently heed the voice of the Lord your God and do what is right in His sight, give ear to His commandments and keep all His statutes, I will put none of the diseases on you which I have brought on the Egyptians. For I am the Lord who heals you"* (Exod. 15:26).

*T*he Lord reveals Himself as the Healer.

## *Jehovah-Rapha*

In another instance of Old Testament healing, the children of Israel became discouraged and again complained against Moses and the Lord. In response to their sin, God sent poisonous serpents into their midst which bit and killed many Israelites (see Num. 21:6). The people repented of their sin and cried out to Moses to save their lives. In answer to Moses's prayer, God provided a strange remedy. He commanded Moses to make a serpent of bronze and place it on a pole. Individuals who were bitten were directed to lift up their eyes and gaze upon the bronze serpent and live. They were healed because of an act of faith (see Num. 21:8-9).

The bronze serpent of Moses is a type of Christ. When we look to Him, He is there for us to save, heal, and deliver. Jesus referred to this Himself while dialoguing with Nicodemus: *"And as Moses lifted up the serpent in the wilderness, even so must the Son of Man be lifted up"* (John 3:14). In the Person of *Jehovah-Rapha*, the Old Testament clearly promises healing.

## *Jehovah-Nissi*

*Jehovah-Nissi* is the name of God revealed to Moses after the Israelites won a great victory against the Amalekites (see Exod. 17:8-16). It is most commonly translated "The Lord Our Banner." The thought here is that of a banner raised by a victorious army, so the Lord is our victory banner. The root word for *nissi* is the word *nes*, however, which means "a standard, banner, flag, sign [and wonder], a miracle." Therefore, a better translation of *Jehovah-Nissi* might be "The Lord our Miracle Worker."[2]

If miraculous healing was in operation under the Old Covenant, how much more is healing available for New Covenant believers today.

If we have a sickness or a fractured bone in our body, we need healing. Generally, when someone receives an instant healing it is called a miracle. However, some healing miracles are so remarkable they are called *creative miracles*. A creative miracle occurs when God does the impossible, such as restoring missing body parts.

In Luke 22:51 Peter drew his sword and cut off the ear of the servant of the high priest. Scripture tells us that Jesus touched the man's ear and healed him. We don't know if Jesus placed the ear on the man's head and it was reattached or if a new ear appeared. However, we do know that it was a great miracle.

> *Jehovah-Nissi is the Lord our Miracle Worker.*

Reflect on the miracle in which Jesus healed a man who was born blind. The man had never seen a single thing (see John 9:1-41). Medical researchers have discovered that using our eyes for vision must be learned during a critical time period in early infant development. The first published case of recovery from blindness from birth was a 13-year-old boy in 1728. The lenses of his eyes had been opaque from birth due to cataracts, but, when the cataracts were removed, the boy could form no judgement about shapes or distinguish any object from another.[3]

A total of 66 early cases of patients who underwent cataract operations were reviewed by Dr. Marius von Senden in a book that was published in German in 1932. It was later translated into English under the title *Space and Sight*.[4] Von Senden noted that shapes, sizes, lengths, and distances are difficult for formerly blind people to judge for a time after their operations.

However, when cataracts were removed from the eyes of individuals who were legally blind from birth, their "sight" failed to be restored. The physical function of the optical system was restored, but not their vision. Although these patients were able to see physically, they couldn't perceive objects as normal people do. They saw only a mixture of confusing colors and shapes that had no meaning for them.

In the Gospel of John, the man who was born blind did not just have diseased eyes, he had a brain untrained to see. Only a miraculous healing indeed could rewire a brain in such a marvelous way! Even at that time, the formerly blind man recognized that he had received an astonishing miracle, a fact that is now scientifically verifiable.

However, the Pharisees, scorning Jesus and the miracle that had just occurred, jeered at the man. Speaking truth that science has now proven, the man who had been born blind retorted: *"Well, this is astonishing! Here a Man has opened my eyes, and yet you do not know where He comes from.... Since the beginning of time it has never been heard that anyone opened the eyes of a man born blind. If this Man were not from God, He would not be able to do anything like this"* (John 9:30-33 AMP). This same Miracle Worker lives in us today!

*T*his same Miracle Worker lives in us today!

# ENDNOTES

1. The tree was a type, or allegorical picture, of the Lord Jesus Christ in His person and work.

2. F. Brown, S.R. Driver, and C.A. Briggs, *The Brown-Driver-Briggs Hebrew and English Lexicon of Old Testament Words*, (Peabody, MA: Hendrickson Publications, 1996), 651.

3. W. Cheselden, "An account of some observations made by a young gentleman, who was born blind, or lost his sight so early, that he had no remembrance of ever having seen, and was couch'd between 13 and 14 years of age," *Philosophical Transactions*, 402 (1727), 447–450.

4. M. von Senden, *Space and Sight: The Perception of Space and Shape in the Congenitally Blind Before and After Operation*, (London: Methuen & Co, 1960).

*Chapter 5*

# ENCOUNTERING THE DIVINE HEALER

Jason and Mandy, friends of ours, and their five children have encountered the Divine Healer...*in their own hearts!* They had already learned how to allow Jesus the forgiver to wash out negative emotions in their hearts and to live in the fruit of the Spirit. Living in the peace of God is a lifestyle for the entire family. Now God began to open up a whole new realm of the miraculous for them.

## A CHILD SHALL LEAD THEM

*Shiri's Story*

It had been a fairly uneventful Sunday, considering. "Nothing like having four younger brothers," Shiri, age 13, thought. "You don't have to worry about quiet or boredom for sure." She brushed a strand of her blonde hair off her forehead and looked around the playroom with all the toys, the chest of clothes for "dress up," the Nerf gun, and the school supplies. But there was no school tomorrow because it was President's Day.

Shiri and her brother, Levi, age 11, were bantering back and forth in playful good humor; however, things suddenly took a bad turn. Levi went from teasing to calling Shiri names. Brothers are like that. Levi didn't mean anything by it, but it's just so much fun to tease your sister. Shiri said, "He made me kinda mad, so we started wrestling! Suddenly Levi kicked his foot up into the air and accidently hit my hand really, really hard!" Whack! "I went on to bed even though it hurt a lot."

"When I got up in the morning it was much worse. I started crying. It was all swollen and it hurt terribly when I tried to bend my hand. I went to find my mom!"

"Uh, oh! This one looks like it could be bad." Shiri's mom, Mandy, wrinkled her brow with concern and said, "I think we need the doctor to take a look at this!" She didn't have to look up the number for the orthopedist; it was already on her phone! Mandy gave the doctor's office a call and told them she was on the way with Shiri. Mandy herded Shiri and her brothers Davey, seven, and Justice, five, into the car and off they zoomed to the doctor's office.

Mandy thought the thumb might be broken. The only way to evaluate whether it was a sprain or fracture was an x-ray. "I thought it was broken because of where Shiri said the pain was located. It was from the top of her wrist to her first thumb knuckle."

On the 30 minute drive to the orthopedist's office, Mandy recalled how she yielded to *Jesus the forgiver* in her heart to release and receive forgiveness. Therefore, she reasoned, "If Jesus the forgiver within is always available to forgive, maybe Jesus the *healer* is also present to heal! I wasn't sure if that would work; it was more of a trial and error thing."

So Mandy said, "Hey, let's try this you guys! Why not apply what we learned so far about forgiveness and see if Jesus the healer will work, too!" So Mandy, Shiri, and her brothers all agreed to give Jesus a try. They applied the same concept of releasing and receiving forgiveness. Shiri yielded to the Divine Healer in her, and everyone else let healing power from Jesus in them flow to Shiri. The pain began to subside. On a scale of one to ten, Shiri's pain level had decreased from a ten to a four.

When they arrived at the doctor's office, Mandy asked Shiri if she wanted to go in or go home and continue to pray. Based on the results Shiri was experiencing, she elected to go home and keep praying.

As soon as they were home, all the children gathered around Shiri and released Jesus the Healer in them to flow out to her while Shiri yielded to the healer in her. As they continued to yield, they evaluated the progress of healing from time to time. The pain continually decreased. While everyone was praying, Davey saw a vision in his spirit of God wrapping gauze around Shiri's thumb and healing it.

Within a few hours, her pain level was all the way down to two; just a little bit of pain was left on her thumb, in between her bottom thumb knuckle and top of her wrist. Mandy says, "Shiri described it as a 'dot,' and I felt that was where the injury occurred."

Shiri prayed again that evening, yielding to Jesus the healer and welcoming healing to flow. She testifies, "Later that night, I was in my room and I dropped down and prayed again. There was still a little pain left in part of my thumb. While I was praying, I suddenly saw (in the spirit) a flash of *light* touch my thumb in the specific area where I still had a little pain. Then the light began to spread out over my thumb and all the soreness left! At this point, I was completely healed."

Mandy later commented, "I know it was the grace of God for my boys to sit and pray that long!"

*And a little child shall lead them* (Isaiah 11:6).

> "*Suddenly* I saw a flash of *light* touch my thumb!"

Jason, Shiri's father, e-mailed us the following testimony:

> Shiri went from having complete immobility to full motion and healing in that day. She has learned, "The wider you open your spirit to Christ the healer, the greater the healing!"

> Now Shiri is practicing opening her heart to allow Jesus the healer to flow out to heal others. Since then, she has participated in this same process with her brothers when they both had injured their ankles. Shiri and Levi were all smiles as his ankle was being healed. It was really

powerful. Shiri knows without a doubt that Jesus can truly heal!

> "*The* wider you open your spirit to
> Christ the healer, the greater the healing!"

### The Divine Healer

If someone asked you where God dwells, would you point toward heaven? Well, you would be correct in one sense because the Scriptures do tell us that a heavenly realm exists where God dwells. The writer of Hebrews tells us, for example, *"For Christ has not entered the holy places made with hands, which are copies of the true, but into heaven itself, now to appear in the presence of God for us"* (Heb. 9:24).

Jesus dwells in the *heart* of every believer through the Holy Spirit. Jesus is not only our Savior. He is also our Immanuel, meaning "God with us" (see Matt. 1:23). He is with us and He is in us. The riches of the kingdom of God are not far off but within us. Scripture says He is *"Christ in you, the hope of glory"* (Col. 1:27). We are God indwelt!

Because the Divine Healer lives in us, His healing power is always available. We don't have to beg for healing power to fall from heaven, but simply yield to Him in our heart and welcome His healing touch into every cell, organ, and system in our physical body.[1]

## *J*esus came to destroy the works of the devil.

Once, when Jesus was ministering at a certain house in Capernaum, people were packed so tightly, both inside and out, that nobody else could even get close to the door (see Mark 2:1-12). It was impossible to get near to Jesus.

Four desperate friends of a paralytic didn't let the crowd stop them, however. With bold faith, they clambered up onto the roof, ripped off tiles, and lowered the bed down through the roof. Jesus immediately told the paralytic that his sins were forgiven. Some scribes who were present were offended and thought, "These are the words of a blasphemer, because only God can forgive sins." (see Mark 2:6) Jesus then said:

> *"Which is easier, to say to the paralytic, 'Your sins are forgiven you,' or to say, 'Arise, take up your bed and walk'? But that you may know that the Son of Man has power on earth to forgive sins"—He said to the paralytic, "I say to you, arise, take up your bed, and go to your house." Immediately he arose, took up the bed, and went out* (Mark 2:8-12).

Notice that *forgiveness* was tied to the subsequent healing of the paralyzed man. Jesus declared that it was just as easy for Him to forgive sins as to heal a paralytic's legs. If Jesus healed then, He is still healing those in need because Jesus *"is the same yesterday, today, and forever"* (Heb. 13:8).

Jason testified of his own need for forgiveness before he could receive healing:

> Since Shiri's healing, we have had other healings occur by yielding to Christ the healer. I had a major spine issue flair up that was excruciatingly painful. In fact, I had a medical professional try to help. It did *some* good, but there was still a lot of pain. I went home and prayed through some emotional issues the Lord was showing me that were related to my back, by allowing Christ the forgiver to release forgiveness through me.
>
> After those prayers, I yielded to Christ the healer and my back was immediately 50 percent better. I could at least sit down without grimacing. The next day I did the same and it got about another 20 to 30 percent better. The rest is slowly healing on its own plus some more medical help. Yielding to Christ the healer did not work at first until I dealt with some of my emotional issues, and then it worked wonderfully. Praise God! Really awesome!

## JESUS THE MIRACLE WORKER

### Levi's Broken Bone Is Healed

In August of 2014, Jason and Mandy's middle son, Levi, age 11, was roughhousing with his brother when he accidently hit him in the face, badly injuring his own hand. The pain was excruciating! Levi yelled and ran upstairs to find his mother.

Crying and worried because of the extreme pain, Levi blurted out, "I might have to go to the hospital!"

Mandy, his mother, examined it. She could feel that a bone on the back of his hand was broken. She says, "It wasn't a full separation, but was definitely a tangible break where I could feel the separation between the two bones." Based on Mandy's observation, and her experience gained from putting many other splints on her children's hurt fingers, she knew this was much worse than usual. Mandy says, "I knew it was more serious than their run-of-the-mill finger fractures."

Mandy did some quick online research about this type of break and discovered that the broken bone was a second metacarpal. She had Levi try to touch his fingers to his palm to make a fist and, as the fingers descended, the middle finger began to overlap the index finger, a *rotational deformity*. This was a bad sign! Mandy had found that, when a finger overlaps another finger by more than ten percent, surgery may be necessary. Screws or pins might be required in such a case.

### Let's Pray!

Mandy quickly realized this went far beyond treating a "common fracture." She told Levi that they could either go to the orthopedist or pray. Being an active child and not too fond of the possibility of screws in his hand, Levi chose to pray. Mandy called all the children together and said, "Okay, let's pray!" Everyone started releasing the healing power of Jesus in them toward Levi while he yielded to Jesus in him. (Mandy later said she felt this healing was faster than Shiri's because everyone was becoming much more proficient in allowing the Lord to rise up within them.)

After an hour, Shiri had to go, but Mandy and Levi continued to pray and stay open to the Lord. They checked Levi's pain level on a scale from one to ten from time to time. It was slowly going down from a ten, to an eight, to a six, to a four. After almost two hours, Mandy and Levi stopped praying and carefully assessed the area. As they paused to look at Levi's hand and examine it, they could see that the middle finger was no longer overlapping his index finger.

Mandy then gently touched the area where the bone had been broken. When she discovered that the pieces of bone had grown back together again (although it still felt soft to the touch), she was in utter amazement. Mandy had never experienced being part of a healing in which she could physically feel the change that had occurred!

> *The* broken pieces of bone
> had grown back together!

The Miracle Worker had healed Levi's hand!

Mandy commented wryly, "We are getting lots of practice praying for healing. With five children, it seems like every couple of weeks someone gets injured!

## THE ANOINTING CALMS
## AN AGGRESSIVE DOG

### Levi Releases the Love of God

One of Levi's friends had a dog that was extremely aggressive, and Levi didn't like being around the dog when he went to his friend's house. When Levi had been there before, the dog had tried to bite him on a couple of occasions. Levi felt like he always had to be on guard around that dog. Levi's dad says:

> Before going over to the friend's house recently, Levi asked his mom what he should do. She replied, "Just pray and release love and peace to the dog." The next time Levi went to visit, he released a flow of love and peace from his heart toward the dog (see John 7:38). Immediately, the dog stopped being aggressive. The whole time Levi was at the house, the dog lay next to him, perfectly calm.
>
> Levi came home and announced, "It worked!" Mandy asked, "What worked?" Levi responded, "I dropped down and released love to the dog and she became calm around me!"
>
> Needless to say, through this occurrence Levi's faith level rose and he realized that "releasing love and peace" can transform the environment.

## FROM UNABLE TO WALK TO PLAYING BASKETBALL

### Benjamin's Story

(Mandy tells the story.) There's another really great story about Benjamin's ankle. Benjamin's incident happened around March of 2014. Benji, age 12, had a basketball tournament game later that day, and it was a really big deal for him.

Our backyard is like "hiking in the woods." It is pretty steep in a lot of areas with water that runs through part of it; it's a lot of climbing up and down hills with a path in the middle. The water is similar to a small creek (really it's runoff from an inlet of the lake, but it is liker to a creek, but not necessarily flowing water). For the most part, the children usually run, play tag, and explore. A while back, they all were building secret forts.

All five kids were out there playing on the day Benji was injured. Benji threw his basketball and scrambled after it as it rolled down a hill. Suddenly, Benji caught his foot under a root and fell, badly wrenching his ankle. We could tell right away something was wrong, more than just a scrape, because Levi dashed frantically to the house to tell us and we could hear the concern in his voice as he shouted, "Benji got hurt!"

It was a Saturday, so Jason was home, and he raced out to find him. He found Benji lying on the ground, not able to stand on his own. Benji was crying and in severe pain. He was also really upset knowing he might have to miss his game. Jason immediately picked him up and carried Benji on his back into the house. When he was on the couch, I removed his shoes. Benji's ankle was already beginning to swell and he was in severe pain. We had recently experienced the healing that had occurred with Shiri's thumb, so we decided to try it again with his ankle.

While icing his ankle, we all sat with him and released healing to his ankle. Although the kids did pray for a while, an hour or so, their attention began to wane because they just spent hours praying for Shiri's thumb a few weeks earlier.

Although the swelling had gone down some and Benji's ankle was better, he was still in pain. Jason, Shiri, and I continued to pray and released the healing power of Jesus to Benji.

Just as we did with Shiri, we assessed the progress of the healing every ten to twenty minutes or so.

At one point, Shiri suggested that Benji open his spirit as wide as he could to the Lord. As he did this, the Lord our healer began flow out of Benjamin to Jason and me in a powerful way! We both began to weep. Our Divine Healer was not only healing Benji, but flowing out of him to touch both of us simultaneously, healing some deep emotional wounds we had been carrying.

The swelling in Benji's ankle went down, the pain subsided, and he was able to play in the basketball game that afternoon.[2]

> *The* Healer began to flow
> out in a powerful way!

Later, Jason and Mandy said they didn't know that the other was experiencing the same type of emotional healing. They described what they had felt as "concentrated flooding" of anointing all over them.

Since this time, various kinds of healings, miracles, and other supernatural happenings have become a regular occurrence in the family. Jason, Mandy, and their five children have also discovered that healing manifests *more and more quickly* the more they *practice* yielding to Him as our Divine Healer in them.

## MORE TESTIMONIES

### Stomach Ailment Healed (Dr. Jen)

Once when Dennis and I were on a ministry circuit, I developed a chronic upset stomach that flared up every time I ate anything at all. While we were riding in the car between meetings, I passed the time by yielding to Christ the healer within, welcoming Him into my digestive system. After a while, Dennis asked me what I was doing, saying that he could discern an increased anointing in my midsection. By the time we had our next meal, my stomach was fine.

### Pain in the Back Healed

A pastor who had read one of our books and knew how to yield to Christ the forgiver for emotional healing shared this testimony of physical healing. One day, his back suddenly went into spasm, and it was accompanied by excruciating pain.

> I am strong and not used to being weak. This was paralyzing. Pain so deep, I could not breathe. Well, if we can yield to Jesus the forgiver, I reasoned that Jesus in me is also the healer. I dropped down into my spirit and I yielded to Christ the healer in me. Within seconds, He ruled over that pain. Healing was immediate. The pain was gone!
> —Daryl, South Carolina

Yielding to Christ the healer within really does work. Christ in us, the hope of glory, is always present, giving life to our spirit, soul, and physical body, whether we need physical healing or forgiveness to flow through us. As we yield to the presence of God within, Christ forgives through us. He also releases His healing power when we yield to the Divine Healer within.

---

### PRACTICE

## SOAK: PRAYER STEP 3

Notice that when you close your eyes to pray, your focus shifts from your head to your spiritual heart in your belly (see John 7:38). Yield to the healing power of Christ within. Welcome God's presence into your physical body.

Soaking requires time and quiet. (You may want to play worship music.)

- **Time.** Set aside a period of time—at least thirty minutes—and wait quietly in the presence of the Divine Healer.
- **Yield.** The more you yield, or open your spirit to God, the faster healing can occur.

---

# ENDNOTES

1. The Greek word *kakos* literally means "evil," but it is often translated "sick." We should not tolerate evil in our physical body, which is the temple of God (see 1 Cor. 6:19-20). Scripture tells us that Jesus came to *destroy* the works of the devil (see 1 John 3:8). Something broken can be mended. However, when something is destroyed, it is ruined beyond repair. Jesus destroyed the power of sin, disease, toxic emotions, death, and everything else that is evil.

2. According to Jason and Mandy, when the boys have been healed of ankle injuries, they discovered that it was best to wait a couple of days before resuming regular activities or a small a bit of pain returned. Benji's ankle started to hurt again during the game so the family prayed again later that day and the pain subsided.

*Chapter 6*

# BRAIN-GUT CONNECTION

I (Jen) was a Christian counselor when I first met Dennis, a pastor, at a conference in Jacksonville, Florida, in 1997. At one of the intercessory prayer meetings, a young woman had an emotional meltdown and ended up crying and writhing on the floor. All 90 intercessors froze and stared but no one attempted to help her. I shook my head in dismay and thought, "Five or ten years of counseling right there on the floor."

Dennis, however, went over to her, knelt down on one knee and started praying with her. Because of my counseling training I knew what was going on. He prayed her through multiple emotional healings and brought down mental strongholds. She automatically received deliverance as open doors that had given the enemy access were being closed. In less than ten minutes she was back on her feet with a smile on her face. I was astounded! I had always been taught that emotional healing via forgiveness was a long process, but this was fast. I thought, "This is huge!"

Immediately I could picture the worldwide church being radically transformed if believers knew these secrets.

My new friendship with Dennis quickly blossomed into romance. Later, when Dennis and I were married, I spent a great deal of time pondering that young woman's rapid healing. Why did Dennis's approach work so quickly and thoroughly compared to everything else I had ever seen? How did it line up theologically? What was the spiritual and physiological mechanism behind such rapid emotional healing?

The answer, as it turns out, lies in how our head and heart are connected.

### *The Location of the Heart*

As Christians, we all would agree that the Bible is our authority on theology. Therefore, we must turn to the actual words used in the Scriptures. What do the Scriptures say about the location of our emotional and spiritual heart, or our "Bible heart"?

As discussed previously, both the Old and New Testaments use words such as *belly* and *bowels* when referring to the heart. In John 7:38, Jesus says, *"He that believeth on Me, as the scripture hath said, out of his belly shall flow rivers of living water"* (KJV). According to *Vine's Expository Dictionary*, "In John 7:38...[belly] stands metaphorically for the innermost part of man, the soul, the heart."[1]

The Bible, therefore, locates the spiritual heart in the belly area, not in the chest! This may go against the tide of conventional thought, but convention is not our source. We would do well to follow the example of the Berean Christians who *"were of more noble character than those in Thessalonica, for they received the message with great eagerness and examined the Scriptures every day to see if what Paul said was true"* (Acts 17:11 NIV).

---

# The Bible locates the spiritual heart in the belly.

---

### The Function of the Heart

Within our heart, we experience the following:

- Grief (see John 14:1; Rom. 9:2; 2 Cor. 2:4).

- Joy (see John 16:22; Eph. 5:19).

- The desires (see Matt. 5:28; 2 Pet. 2:14).

- The affections (see Luke 24:32; Acts 21:13).

- The perceptions (see John 12:40; Eph. 4:18).

- The thoughts (see Matt. 9:4; Heb. 4:12).

- The understanding (see Matt. 13:15; Rom. 1:21).

- The reasoning powers (see Mark 2:6; Luke 24:38).

- The imagination (see Luke 1:51).

- The conscience (see Acts 2:37; 1 John 3:20).

- The intentions (see Heb. 4:12; 1 Pet. 4:1).

- Purpose (see Acts 11:23; 2 Cor. 9:7).

- The will (see Rom. 6:17; Col. 3:15).

- Faith (see Mark 11:23; Rom. 10:10; Heb. 3:12).

As we can see, the belly is the location of our entire emotional and spiritual heart-life. Our human spirit fills us head to toe; however, we connect with God spirit-to-Spirit when we open the door in our heart. The *anointing* from Christ within flows out from the belly. The Bible locates the epicenter of our *spirit* in the belly. The spirit is the sphere of divine influence, or the lamp of the Lord. The writer of Proverbs said, *"The spirit of man is the candle of the Lord, searching all the inward parts of the belly"* (Prov. 20:27 KJV).

Our *emotional heart* is also found in the belly. Love and compassion flow from the belly. *"Joseph made haste; for his bowels did yearn upon his brother: and he sought where to weep; and he entered into his chamber, and wept there"* (Gen. 43:30 KJV). And Paul wrote the church at Philippi: *"For God is my record, how greatly I long after you all in the bowels* [affection] *of Jesus Christ"* (Phil. 1:8 KJV). Wounds of the heart are also located in the belly: *"The words of a talebearer are as wounds, and they go down into the innermost parts of the belly"* (Prov. 18:8 KJV).

### *The Door of the Heart*

According to Revelation 3:20, our heart has a *door*. When you got saved, did you ask Jesus to come into your head or your heart? You opened the door of your *heart* to Him. The door is in our heart, not our head. Salvation is a *heart relationship,* not a mental philosophy.

The door of the heart can open and close. The door of the heart is actually our *will.* We opened the door of our heart to

Jesus at the time of salvation. We must *keep* the door open for fellowship. If we close the door to Christ within, we are *in the flesh*. When we open the door to Christ within, we are *in the Spirit*. Paul warns the Galatians about this very thing: *"Are you so foolish and so senseless and so silly? Having begun [your new life spiritually] with the [Holy] Spirit, are you now reaching perfection [by dependence] on the flesh?"* (Gal. 3:3 AMP).

*T*he door of our heart is our will.

How many areas of life should the Spirit rule? Every single one! All things concerning our life—our thoughts, will, emotions, relationships, possessions, finances, and our physical body—should be under the control of the Holy Spirit. That is what is meant by the Lordship of Jesus Christ.

### Drop Down to the Spirit

When we drop down to our spirit, we shift our focus from *head* to *heart*. Our head can know *about* God but only our heart can truly *know* God. When I (Dennis) was a young Christian, I mentored a brilliant Harvard student in the things of God. After I had worked with him for a couple of years, he presented me with a new Bible in which he had inscribed, "To Dennis: You taught me that the education of the mind comes through much study, but the education of the heart comes only by the anointing of God."

As soon as we *drop down* to our spirit and focus on Christ within, the door of our heart *opens* to Jesus. Unless we get out of our head and open our heart to Christ within, we can't connect with God spirit-to-Spirit. We must meet Him in the Spirit, not in our flesh. If we *focus* on something, we pay attention to it. Whether or not we are aware of it, most of the time our focus shifts from head to heart when we close our eyes to pray.

---

*W*hen we drop down to our
spirit, we open to Jesus.

---

When we open the door of our heart, we make a spiritual connection with God. As previously mentioned, focusing on Christ within is like dropping a bucket down a well to draw up water. The prophet Isaiah confirms this: *Therefore with joy will you draw water from the wells of salvation* (Isaiah 12:3). Remember, there's no living water in our head!

---

*T*here's no living water in our head!

---

### The Second Brain

Based on what the Scriptures say, we have learned that the center of our *spiritual life* is located in the gut. Science also informs us that our *emotional heart* is centered in the same location. Have you ever heard bad news and felt "sick" in your gut? You listened to the words, reacted emotionally, and felt it in your gut. Most of us have felt "butterflies" in our belly when we were excited. Children often report having a "tummy ache" when they are emotionally upset.

In 1999, a gastroenterologist named Dr. Michael Gershon published a groundbreaking book called *The Second Brain*.[2] He had made some discoveries in his research that created quite a stir in the scientific community. Dr. Gershon discovered another nervous system, the *enteric nervous system*. We have a separate nervous system in our gut in addition to the central nervous system (the brain, spinal cord, and peripheral nerves). This research birthed a new branch of biology called *psychoneuroimmunology*.

In early embryonic development, a band of neuroectodermal cells, called the neural crest, divides. Over a three-week period of time, approximately 86 billion cells migrate extensively and form the brain, spinal cord, and peripheral nerves. Another 200 to 600 million migrate to the gut and line the esophagus, stomach, small intestine, and colon. A relatively small number, 40 thousand, migrate to the physical heart to regulate its beat. It is important to note that the physical heart does not relay any emotional information to the brain. It simply responds to the emotional information it receives from the gut and limbic system.

> *The brain in our gut tells the brain in our head how we feel!*

The left vagus nerve extends from the emotional center of the brain, making a connection between the brain and gut. The brain doesn't relay information to the gut, however. The enteric nervous system informs our brain. In other words, the brain in our gut tells the brain in our head how we feel!

The enteric nervous system functions as an autonomous entity. The second brain can learn, remember, and function independently of the head brain.

What purposes does the second brain serve? It works in tandem with the immune system and controls digestion. We find 80 to 95 percent of all serotonin (the molecule of happiness) in the gut. Serotonin regulates sleep, appetite, and mood.

The second brain also controls our *emotional climate*. It relays emotional information to the brain in the head as well as our entire body via the left vagus nerve and the release of *neuropeptides*, the molecules of emotion. Scientists have discovered that the gut is a repository of emotional information, determining our emotional health or lack thereof. This is why our digestive tract is so sensitive to emotions and most gastrointestinal diseases are due to emotional distress.

Scientists are not the only ones who have understood the brain gut connection. Long before modern science, a famous theologian shed light on the matter. Jonathan Edwards (1703–1758) was a preacher, theologian, missionary to Native Americans, and considered to be the father of the First Great Awakening in America (1730–1760). Based on what he observed during revival, Edwards asserted that the emotions are the gateway to knowing God.

Edwards penned his 1746 text, *A Treatise Concerning Religious Affections,* in defense of heart versus head Christianity at a time when many clergymen objected to emotional displays due to spiritual experiences. According to Edwards, unless the emotions were deeply affected, he could see little or no evidence of spiritual transformation in the lives of individuals. Mental assent, it seems, did not produce true belief.[3]

Commenting on 1 Peter 1:8 (KJV)—*"Whom having not seen, ye love; in whom, though now you see Him not, yet believing, ye rejoice with joy unspeakable and full of glory"*—he writes, "The proposition, or doctrine, that I would raise from these words, is this: ...True religion, in great part, consists in holy affections."[4] He went on to explain that the affections are "the most vigorous and sensible exercises of the inclination and will of the soul."[5]

In addition, Edwards observed that emotions controlled the will, whether they were carnal passions or the supernatural fruit of the Spirit, or holy affections. Inclination, as defined by Edwards, is emotional preference or aversion to a particular thing wedded to the choices of the will—but at its core, the motivation is emotional. Inclination, therefore, inseparably connects will and emotion, thus impelling behavior through "liking or disliking, [being] pleased or displeased, [or] approving or rejecting."[6] Therefore, even though he was one of America's greatest thinkers, Edwards understood that the emotions played a vital role in one's relationship with the Lord.

### *The Problem: The Feeling-Thought Loop*

Have you ever heard of a *feedback loop*? When we eat, for example, our pancreas produces increased insulin. As our food is digested, our pancreas receives a signal to lower insulin production and the level drops. Every time we eat, the sequence is repeated. It is a "closed process" that operates again and again in an automatic fashion.

Another feedback loop, a *feeling-thought* loop, connects our head and heart. It is impossible to separate our emotions from our thoughts. They are inextricably linked together in feeling-thought bundles, or *emo-cognitions,* which in turn motivate our choices. Emotions rule both our thoughts and our will. We are wired as an indivisibly linked system!

> *I*t is impossible to separate our thoughts from our emotions!

Activity within the feedback loop is beyond our control. That explains the struggle described in Romans 7—we find ourselves failing to do those things we want to do and doing what we don't want to do. When something is linked in the loop, it is out of our control. It defies all our attempts to change. Even when we try to do something differently, what goes on in the loop is stronger than our willpower.

When our "buttons" get pushed, we react. That same button will elicit the same reaction time and time again. Your feeling-thought loop gets activated and the same thought and negative emotion pop up each time. To deal with the button, you have to get inside the loop. If we don't break into the loop somehow, we are trapped in cycles that just keep happening over and over again.

### The Solution: Getting God in the Loop

How then can change happen? Is it impossible? Certainly not! However, it requires something outside the loop breaking into the loop to change what is operating within the system.

At the time of salvation, we opened the door of our heart and invited Jesus to come in the door. In other words, when we got saved, God got in the loop. We began thinking new thoughts, making different choices, and experiencing God's emotions (the fruit of the Spirit). That is how we are supposed to live the Christian life.

To walk in the Spirit, we must keep the door of the heart open to Christ within to maintain our connection with Him (see John 15:5). The secret for living in the Spirit is *keeping* God in the loop. He is in the loop when our heart is *open,* or joined to Him. The Bible says, *"He who is joined to the Lord is one spirit with Him"* (1 Cor. 6:17).

How does this operate in relation to prayer, forgiveness, and emotional healing? When we open the door of our heart in prayer, the love of God can flow into our whole being, including our feeling-thought loop. If the door of our heart is open to God, all we have to do to forgive or be forgiven is to present our heart to Christ the forgiver and allow Him to forgive in and through us. When God gets in the loop, He can heal our emotional wounds, influence our thoughts, and govern our choices. If we fail to allow God into the loop, we live in carnality.

Does the Bible have anything to say about the matter? Yes! David prayed, *"Search me, O God, and know my heart; try me and know my anxious thoughts; and see if there be any hurtful way in me, and lead me in the everlasting way"* (Ps. 139:23-24 NASB). What are "anxious thoughts" and "hurtful ways"? An anxious thought is an emo-cognition, while a hurtful way is an emo-volition. Emotions rule our thoughts; emotions rule our will.

The most common approach in traditional therapy, both secular and Christian, is to attempt to force the thoughts to control the emotions. Counselors and therapists try to break into the feeling-thought feedback loop via thoughts. They realize that if they can't adjust the operation of the feedback loop, no change will occur.

However, it appears that the thoughts may not be the best place to begin after all. Joseph LeDoux, author of *The Emotional Brain*, says the aim of psychoanalysis is to get the thoughts (cortex) to gain control of the emotions. But he admits this is a difficult and prolonged process.[7] Perhaps we shouldn't start with the thoughts at all. Could change occur more easily if we *started* with the emotions themselves by going through the door of the heart, just as Jesus suggests? Yes. God's way is easier, better, and faster!

Lasting transformation must begin in the heart and it always starts with the emotions. The good news is that, when we connect with God in prayer, we have already let Him in the loop. When we open our heart in prayer, our emotions can be presented to God. We don't have to tolerate toxic emotions. Forgiveness is the antidote!

> *W*hen we start with the emotions,
> God gets into the loop.

As soon as God is in the loop, He can forgive through us. Christ the forgiver lives inside us. We don't *try* to forgive; we simply yield to Christ the forgiver in our heart and allow Him to forgive through us. That is the secret of forgiveness. When we start with the emotions, God gets in the loop and He brings transformation to feeling-thoughts and feeling-choices. We must allow the Lord to do the work of changing our emotions, thoughts, and choices, because only God can transform us!

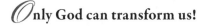

*O*nly God can transform us!

## ENDNOTES

1. Vine, *Vine's Expository Dictionary,* 118.

2. M. Gershon, *The Second Brain: A Groundbreaking New Understanding of Nervous Disorders of the Stomach and Intestine,* (New York, NY; Harper Collins, 2003).

3. Jonathan Edwards, *A Treatise Concerning Religious Affections,* (New York, NY: Cosimo Classics, 2007). The back cover text of this edition sums up Edwards's main arguments throughout: "How do we discern between true religion, and false? In this classic treatise on the nature of authentic faith, enormously influential American preacher and theologian Jonathan Edwards (1703–1758) explores the difference between true and counterfeit religious experiences, and how deep and sincere emotion can accentuate a real connection to God."

4. Ibid. 9.

5. Ibid.

6. Ibid.

7. J. LeDoux, *The Emotional Brain: The Mysterious Underpinnings of Emotional Life,* (New York, NY: Simon and Schuster, 1996), 303.

*Chapter 7*

# EMOTIONS: THE LANGUAGE OF THE CELLS

On a warm spring day in 1991, an intriguing flyer arrived in the mail. It announced an upcoming women's conference on *the joy of the Lord*. I (Jen) had always been taught that the fruit of the Spirit grew as the result of godly character. But how could you actually tell if you had any? It seemed very mysterious, but I wanted it. So, I registered for the conference right away. Of course, it didn't hurt that the venue was a beautiful resort on the coast of southern Georgia. What a combination—beach, lovely hotel, springtime, and...joy!

The conference turned out to be a big disappointment, though. The speakers taught what the Bible said *about* joy for the most part. One woman said she had experienced supernatural joy once, even though she was going through a rough time in her life, but didn't know how she got "it" or if she would ever have joy again. Apparently no one had joy or knew how to get it! This was very discouraging. Was the fruit of the Spirit just a mental concept with no experience?

I didn't learn anything else about joy until 1997, after Dennis and I were married. It was wonderful news to discover that he had the very answers I was looking for. One of the first evenings we prayed together, he asked me to close my eyes and get in an attitude of prayer. Next, he told me to put my hand on my belly and yield to Christ within.

Dennis then told me to pay attention to what I was *feeling* and asked, "Tell me how you feel. Is it different from just talking or thinking about something?"

"Why, yes," I said. "It feels sort of like what I feel in a worship service! So this must be the presence of God!"

"That's the peace of God," Dennis explained. "Now yield even more." As I did, a smile came to my face. I could feel a bubble of joy inside. Dennis said, "What you're feeling now is *joy*. That's the joy of the Lord!"

I opened my eyes in astonishment. "Do you mean we can tap into the fruit of the Spirit as easily as we can yield to Christ the forgiver in us? And we can have a *real* experience?"

"*Yes!* When we are in the presence of God, we feel the *fruit* of His presence."

"*He Himself is our peace*" (Eph. 2:14), and, "*The joy of the Lord is* [our] *strength*" (Neh. 8:10).

### Why Did God Give Us Emotions?

Why did God create us with emotions in the first place? Emotions were meant to be conduits of *supernatural emotions*—God's emotions or the fruit of the Spirit. When we are born again, we have access to the supernatural emotions of God.

We make our peace with God and Jesus gives us His peace as a gift (see John 14:27). God is love and He has deposited His love in our heart: *"The love of God has been poured out in our hearts by the Holy Spirit who was given to us"* (Rom. 5:5). And Scripture commands us to be joyful and *"rejoice in the Lord always. Again I will say, rejoice!"* (Phil 4:4). We can't tap into something we don't have. Therefore, we already have the joy of the Lord in us.

> *We* have access to the supernatural emotions of God.

The fruit of the Spirit is *evidence* that the kingdom of God is at hand: *"For the kingdom of God is...righteousness and peace and joy in the Holy Spirit"* (Rom. 14:17). When Jesus rules, righteousness, peace, and joy are *evidence* His kingdom has come.

When we have love, peace, and joy in our heart, we know we're operating out of the right kingdom: *"The kingdom of God is within"* (Luke 17:21). The love chapter of the Bible, 1 Corinthians 13, describes how we should allow God's love to work through us: *"Love is patient, love is kind"* (1 Cor. 13:4 NASB). Paul writes in regard to the fruit of the Spirit: *"The fruit of the Spirit is love, joy, peace, patience, kindness, goodness, faithfulness, gentleness, self-control; against such things there is no law"* (Gal. 5:22-23 NASB). Notice that the word *fruit* is singular. Love is *one fruit.* In Galatians 5:22-23, the love of God is described as one fruit with nine different expressions.

### One Fruit: Love

- Joy is love rejoicing

- Peace is love resting

- Patience is love enduring

- Kindness is love caring

- Goodness is love motivating

- Faithfulness (faith) is love trusting

- Gentleness is love esteeming others (see Phil. 1:3)

- Self-control is love restraining (power under control)

*But we all, with unveiled face, beholding as in a mirror the glory of the Lord, are being transformed into the same image from glory to glory, just as by the Spirit of the Lord* (2 Corinthians 3:18).

> The fruit of the Spirit is one
> fruit with nine expressions.

### Origin of Negative Emotions

In the Garden of Eden, before Adam and Eve sinned, the spiritual atmosphere was flooded with the glory and love of

God. Prior to sin entering the picture, Adam and Eve only experienced God's emotions. In such an atmosphere, they only knew health. The Garden was a frontier outpost of heaven brought to earth. Just as in heaven, the presence and glory of God were there and His good and loving will ruled His creation. A banner, or flag, is an emblem of victory signifying the governing authority or kingdom ruling over a particular territory or nation. God raised His banner of love in the Garden and reigned over His kingdom on earth.

However, the perfection didn't last. In a few short verses in the Book of Genesis we read that sin soon separated Adam and Eve from God's kingdom of love, and they experienced toxic emotions for the very first time. Lust created a desire for forbidden fruit and Eve feared that God was withholding something good. After eating the fruit, Adam and Eve were afraid and hid from God. They felt guilt and the shame of nakedness. Adam became angry and blamed Eve (see Gen. 3:1-24). After the Fall, every part of Adam and Eve's being became vulnerable to attack—spirit, soul, and body. The voice of their emotions, which had only proclaimed health and life before, now began to speak disease and death.

> *God* raised His banner of love in the Garden.

The devil's kingdom is a kingdom of fear. The enemy began to plant the flags of his kingdom in the gardens of their hearts. Wherever he planted them, he gained the legal right to bring torment into their lives. Adam and Eve were no longer in harmony with God nor one another. When emotions were no longer under the control of the Spirit, they came under the rule of carnal emotions, both good and bad. No sickness had ever existed before toxic emotions. Now their bodies were doomed to die.

When we yield to God's emotions, the fruit of the Spirit, we move into a heavenly realm far surpassing human emotion. We can experience the same spiritual and emotional climate that was in the Garden. The love of God is the most powerful force in the universe, and we have been given the privilege to be saturated with His love.

In one of His messages to the seven churches in the book of Revelation, Jesus admonishes the church at Ephesus to return to first love (see Rev. 2:4). First love is not the immature and somewhat selfish love of a new believer. It is the perfect love that first existed in the Garden between Father God and His son and daughter, Adam and Eve.

For those who overcome and return to first love, Jesus promises that He will "grant to eat" of the fruit "of the tree of life, which is in the paradise of God" (Rev. 2:7). We will have access to the very fruit and paradise atmosphere forfeited by Adam and Eve.

*The voice of our emotions speaks to our body.*

### Open the Gates

Throughout the history of humankind, God has reached out to us. He created us with the capacity to respond to His love in every way—spirit, soul, and body. Our spirit and soul encounter God via the door of our heart. How do our cells encounter the love of God? Our cells have gates that can open and close. The cell membrane is semi-permeable with protein *openings* allowing transport into and out of the cell. *Gates and channels* (receptors and effectors) allow the cell to receive, or absorb, what is in the surrounding environment.[1]

## Cell Membrane

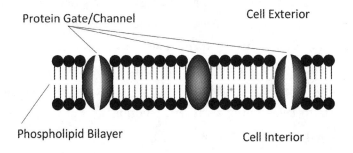

Protein Gate/Channel     Cell Exterior

Phospholipid Bilayer     Cell Interior

When our cells encounter the power of God, the gates open and receive the glory of God. Our body understands the meaning of: *"Lift up your heads, O you gates! And be lifted up, you everlasting doors! And the King of glory shall come in"* (Ps. 24:7). When you are in the presence of God, welcome Him to enter the gates of your cells.

*W*elcome the King of glory into your cells!

## Cellular Resonance

Neuropeptides, the molecules of emotion, are one of a variety of small molecules called ligands that bind specifically to cellular receptors and transmit information received to the cell. The surfaces of most cells have hundreds of thousands of different receptors. A typical nerve cell may have millions on its surface. In other words, molecules of emotion inform our nerves about our emotional state.

A ligand has been described as a chemical key that fits into a cellular keyhole—the receptor. When the key is inserted into its perfectly designed keyhole (the receptor), the lock is opened, binding occurs, and information enters the cell. Scientists now prefer to describe the process as a more active, vibratory attraction. Therefore, the cell membrane is in a continual state of flux. In the case of emotional signaling, the neuropeptide and receptor begin to vibrate to the same frequency in a manner similar to two tuning forks. An emotional "chord" is struck whenever they bind together.

## A Community of Cells

Whereas single-cell organisms "read" environmental cues directly and modify their behavior accordingly, cells in the human body live in a community of cells, requiring communication for cooperation. In community, specialized cells of the nervous and immune system bring the individual cells under the authority of a "common plan of action." For example, the immune system is designed to fight off invaders who attack within the organism rather than each cell having to defend itself in isolation.

In higher life forms, the brain has a specialized mechanism that enables our cells, systems, and organs to cooperate. The central nervous system and brain coordinate specialized "signal molecules" to maintain oversight of the whole organism. Cells yield their autonomy to the coordination of the brain. Molecules of emotion keep the individual cells informed and synchronized, but the brain presides over the community.

An organism's ability to maintain a constant internal balance is called *homeostasis*. Negative emotions, however, can disrupt the balance of our "community of cells" and set the stage for physical illness. Sickness and disease indicate that there are parts of our body not cooperating with the well-being of the community.

---

*A*s God heals the emotions, the
Holy Spirit is free to heal our body.

---

How do we process emotional information? Candace Pert, author of *The Molecules of Emotion*, found that the same information-processing neural receptors present on nerve cell membranes are present on most, if not all, of the body's cells. What does this mean? Our "mind" is not focused in our head exclusively, but is distributed via signal molecules to the entire body.[2]

"The mind as we experience it is immaterial, yet it has a physical substrate, which is both body and brain. It may also be said to have a nonmaterial, nonphysical substrate that has to do with the flow of that information."[3] We can, therefore, think of mind and consciousness in terms of emotional information processing, which is *independent* of both brain and body.

### Moods and the Immune System

An emotion is fleeting. We can't make an emotion and we can't maintain any emotion for very long. However, a mood can last for days, weeks, months, or years. Why is this? Moods can change the brain itself. In 1982, Dr. Ed Blalock discovered that our immune system cells secrete peptides. Our immune system *makes* molecules of emotion. "The idea that there were brain peptides in the immune system was so unsettling to immunologists that Blalock's work was not believed at first."[4]

Blalock had made two key discoveries. The first was that molecules of emotions breach the "blood-brain barrier," thus keeping our brain constantly informed about our emotional state.[5]

Blaock's second discovery was that immune cells don't just have emotion receptors. They also "make, store and secrete the neuropeptides themselves. In other words, the immune cells are making the same chemicals that we conceive of as controlling mood in the brain.

Over time, moods can alter the structure of our brain.[6] For example, chronic depression is a mood, not just an emotion. If a person stays in a depressed mood for a long time (unremitting depression), there is good evidence that some parts of the brain change their activity and certain areas of the brain itself may atrophy.

So, immune cells not only control the tissue integrity of the body, but they also manufacture information chemicals that can *regulate* mood or emotion.[7]"

In short, our immune system makes hormones controlling our overall mood. A depressed mood indicates that our immune system is depressed. A peaceful mood enhances the proper functioning of our immune system. This is why our emotions can influence our immunity to certain diseases. It explains why people who are depressed, in emotional turmoil, or live in a state of chronic stress often have a suppressed immune system, too.

The main enemies of our immune system are toxic emotions and stress. The cells of our immune system travel throughout our body to repair and defend it. If our immune system is not functioning properly, it can't restore what needs to be repaired, nor can it kill what needs to be destroyed.

How we view ourselves is closely tied to how the immune system functions. The immune system is designed to protect us. However, when we make judgments against ourselves we can cause our immune system to turn on us and begin to harm our body. Allergies and autoimmune conditions are two examples of the correlation between self-incrimination and damage done to our body an immune system gone rogue.

> *The* main enemies of our immune
> system are toxic emotions and stress.

What is the good news? God can change us inside and out! Research indicates that prayer produces quantifiable positive effects on both our immune system and brain.[8] Every time we are in the presence of God, at least some healing occurs.[9] When we pray regularly, we create a healing environment for our body. We become less likely to become sick and also recover more quickly from surgery and illness.

### Love or Fear

In the natural, emotions can be divided into two classes—love-based and fear-based. Love-based emotions promote good health, and fear-based emotions produce poor health. In the kingdom of God, we encounter a third class of emotions—*supernaturally good emotions*!

When we experience emotions, signal molecules bombard the *cells of the body* with emotional communication. The emotions are the intercom system of the body that communicates life or death to all the cells, organs, and systems of the physical body. For example, the emotion of *love* speaks "life and security" to our cells while the emotion of *fear* says "death and danger." We must ask ourselves, "What am I telling the cells of my body through my emotions?" Since God didn't give you fear, don't take it! Receive forgiveness for taking in fear and welcome the love of God to replace it.

> *God did not give us a spirit of timidity* (of cowardice, of craven and cringing and fawning fear), *but [He has given us a spirit] of power and of love and of calm and well-balanced mind and discipline and self-control* (2 Timothy 1:7 AMP).

*€*motions are the intercom system of the body.

## The Science of Love

It was once believed that the brain of a child was *plastic*, or moldable, while that of an adult was with fixed and immutable neuronal circuits we know that the brain has lifelong plasticity. "Plasticity allows us to develop brains so unique—in response to our individual life experiences—that it is often hard to see the world as others do, want what they want, or cooperate with others."[10]

Fortunately, *oxytocin*, the molecule of love and attachment, gives us the opportunity to open emotional doors to one another and form close relationships, thereby overriding personal idiosyncrasies. As it turns out, the brain is an organ of socialization, and oxytocin is the chemical that creates the ability for humans to form social bonds. Oxytocin, also known as the "cuddle hormone," encourages relational bonding. It induces a peaceful mood, increases tender feelings, strengthens emotional attachments, encourages generosity, and causes us to trust.

As a *neuromodulator*, or brain changer, oxytocin rearranges the "mapping" of the brain and creates *neural pathways* of relationship. Along with *hearts* making a connection with another person, *brains* also have the ability to merge separate lifestyles into one. Love is not only a feeling; it is a biological reality.

## The Love of God

"Massive neuronal reorganization occurs at two life stages: when we fall in love and when we begin parenting."[11] A third instance of extensive reorganization in both our spiritual and physical life occurs at the time of salvation. We are changed spiritually, but in the process oxytocin changes us physically. When we welcome Jesus into our heart, the natural molecules of love merge with the *supernatural* love of God. The love of God floods our feeling-thought loop, transforming our thoughts, will, and emotions. Thereafter, each time we connect with God in prayer, our spirit, soul, and body are changed by His love.

Oxytocin has one other property that is highly significant for believers. It allows unlearning to take place so that our view of ourselves can change for the better in the presence of an adoring partner. When we begin to see ourselves through God's eyes, we are changed. How does God see us? God sees us through eyes of love. We are the center of His attention and the apple of His eye!

> *Behold what manner of love the Father has bestowed on us, that we should be called children of God!* (1 John 3:1).

*W*hen we begin to see ourselves through God's eyes, we are changed.

### Emotions Are Our Friends

Consider this description of the kingdom of God in Romans 14:17 again:

> *The kingdom of God is...righteousness and peace and joy in the Holy Spirit.*

It is clear that two of the words used to describe God's kingdom are emotional. We know that peace and joy are emotions, but what about righteousness? It is emotional too, because righteousness may be defined as "the love of God in action." God is love and love is the source of everything done by God. Taking a closer look, however—what about righteousness? Righteousness is obedience to God or "love in action." Therefore, the kingdom of God is expressed in terms of emotion. This should not be surprising because God is, after all, an emotional God. God does not just *have* love; He *is* love (see 1 John 4:8).

At the time of salvation, God delivers us *"from the power of darkness"* and conveys us *"into the kingdom of the Son of His love"* (Col. 1:13). He rescues us from darkness and makes us citizens of His kingdom. Emotions are friends that alert us if we take a detour into the wrong kingdom. Whenever we experience any emotion that doesn't have the nature of God on it, we know we have entered enemy territory. Forgiveness always takes us back into God's territory and restores the peace of God.

### Emotional Beings

The most famous statement ever made by French philosopher René Descartes (1596–1650) was, "I *think*, therefore I am." He was wrong. We are *emotional beings* who think. Our *heart* rules our *head*, not the other way around. According to neuroscientist Joseph LeDoux, "Our emotions influence every...aspect of our...life, shaping our perceptions, memories, thoughts, and dreams."[12]

*I feel*, therefore I am.

## PRACTICE
### REMOVE SELF-JUDGMENTS

To find the roots of self-judgment, get in an attitude of prayer and ask the Lord to show you when you judged yourself or believed judgments someone else made against you.

*First-Feel-Forgive*

* **Pray.** Close your eyes and pray, placing your hand on your belly.

* **Inquire.** Ask, "Where did I judge myself?"

* **First.** Focus on the first situation that comes to mind.

* **Feel.** Allow yourself to feel the negative emotion momentarily.

* **Forgive.** Yield to Christ the forgiver within. Allow a river of forgiveness to flow toward another person or receive it for yourself until you feel peace.

* **Fact.** After forgiving and getting peace, if there is a negative thought or lie, renounce the lie out loud. Next, ask the Lord for the truth (scriptural fact) and receive it in your heart. Truth rises up from your spirit and informs your mind.

## TROUBLESHOOTING
### DEALING WITH LIES

**Fact.** A lie may come in at the time of emotional wounding. In an attitude of prayer, ask the Lord to show you where it got started in your life. For example, *"My mother was always sick so I'm afraid I'll always be sick."*

* **Pray.** Close your eyes and pray, placing your hand on your belly.
* **First:** Allow the Lord to show you where the thought came in.
* **Feel.** Feel the feeling momentarily.
* **Forgive.** Forgive or receive forgiveness until you feel peace.
* **Fact.**
  * **Renounce.** Renounce any negative thought out loud.
  * **Welcome truth.** Ask God for the truth and welcome it into your heart.

# ENDNOTES

1. Lipton, *The Biology of Belief,* 86.

2. Pert, *The Molecules of Emotion,* 185.

3. Ibid., 180.

4. J.E. Blalock, "The Immune System as the Sixth Sense," *Journal of Internal Medicine* Vol. 257, no. 2 (February 2005), 126–138; J.E. Blalock, "The Immune System as a Sensory Organ," *Journal of Immunology* 132 (1984), 1067–1070.

5. "Brain-immune system interactions: Relevance to the pathophysiology and treatment of neuropsychiatric disorders," *The American Psychiatric Publishing Textbook of Psychopharmacology*, 4th Edition, Psychiatry

Online, Retrieved September 4, 2014 from http://
www.psychiatryonline.org/doi/full/10.1176/appi.books
.9781585623860.as09.

6.  V. Maxwell, "Depression, Chemistry, and Circumstance:
    A Tricky Intersection," *Psychology Today* (February
    28, 2014). Retrieved May 4, 2014 from https://
    www.psychologytoday.com/blog/crazy-life/201402/
    depression-chemistry-and-circumstance.

7.  Blalock, "The Immune System as the Sixth Sense"; Blalock,
    "The Immune System as a Sensory Organ."

8.  D. Matthews and C. Clark, *The Faith Factor: Proof of the
    Healing Power of Prayer*, (New York, NY: Penguin Group
    USA, Inc., 1998), 60–82.

9.  R.J. Davidson, et al., "Alterations in brain and immune
    function produced by mindfulness meditation," *Psychosomatic
    Medicine* 65, no. 4 (July-August 2003), 564–570.

10. N. Doidge, T*he Brain That Changes Itself: Stories of Personal
    Triumph from the Frontiers of Brain Science,* (New York, NY:
    Penguin Books, 2007), 120-121.

11. Ibid., 118.

12. LeDoux, *The Emotional Brain,* 12.

*Chapter 8*

# THE FRUIT OF PEACE

Let's take a closer look at the *supernatural peace* Jesus has given to us as a gift: *"Peace I leave with you, My peace I give to you"* (John 14:27). Jesus makes His peace available for *us* to enjoy! In English, the word *peace* is usually understood as tranquility or a lack of conflict. The peace of God, however, is so much more than that. Peace is authority. Peace is power. Peace is kingdom. When we learn to live in peace as a lifestyle, we should regularly experience God's miraculous intervention on our behalf.

Jen and I (Dennis) were doing some itinerant ministry in the New England states a number of years ago. One night we were returning from a long day of meetings; it was getting late. We were very tired but knew that when we exited I-91 onto I-84 we would be only one exit away from our hotel. As we got to the top of the ramp, we suddenly realized that the traffic on the interstate was at a complete standstill. No one could move forward and some cars were even attempting to turn around and go down the up ramps. As we watched in dismay, we could see policemen putting yellow crime scene tape all the way across the highway on both sides. Uh, oh! This didn't look promising at all. As soon as we noticed tension in our guts, however, we released the whole situation into the hands of God and got our peace back. As soon as we had our peace restored, the following events transpired:

> Inexplicably, I felt led to move one car length over, which is ridiculous with hundreds of stalled cars all around us. I didn't think, "I'm going to change lanes." I was paying more attention to my gut than my head. I wasn't looking for a second opinion—I was looking for God's opinion.
>
> When I pulled the car into the other lane, we were right next to the concrete median wall where the tape was attached. Almost immediately a police-man came and pulled back the tape, allowing eight or nine cars to pass through, then he put the tape back, stopping traffic once again. Our car was the last one to go through. We heard on the news the following day that the highway was closed until 6:00 a.m. because the police were looking for shell casings from a shootout that started in Hartford and continued as the perpetrators roared down the expressway.
>
> It was such a supernatural event. We believe the officer might have been an angel who opened the way and let us through that night.[1]

*And we know that all things work together for good to those who love God, to those who are the called according to His purpose* (Romans 8:28).

When we honor God even in the midst of difficult circumstance, we take the kingdom stance of peace. When we have peace, we are in the river of God's will and, without fail, He will turn messes into miracles. We honored God by choosing the peace of His kingdom, and He blessed us out of the bounty of His goodness: *"Those who honor Me I will honor"* (1 Sam. 2:30).

Some time ago, I (Jen) woke up on what promised to be an ordinary day. However, when I looked at myself in the mirror, I was alarmed to see that I looked like something out of a horror because my eyes were bright red. Not a little bit red but seriously red! What on earth was going on? There was no itching, burning, or discomfort but my appearance was alarming.

An ophthalmologist informed me that my eyes were "massively inflamed." Furthermore, he could find no evidence of a medical condition such as conjunctivitis or an environmental explanation (such as an allergic reaction). It was very mysterious. Reluctantly, the doctor prescribed what he called "the big guns," extremely powerful steroid eye drops that can only be used short-term. Potential damaging side effects included glaucoma and the formation of cataracts.

When I considered the possibility of batteries of tests and multiple appointments I began to feel anxious. As soon as I came home, Dennis had me receive forgiveness for giving in to fear and then welcome the presence of the Divine Healer into my eyes. As soon as my peace was restored, healing happened.

To this day, we have no idea what caused the inflammation. However, we do know that peace includes healing and health.

In *shalom,* Hebrew for "peace", we have completeness, wholeness, health, peace, welfare, safety, soundness, tranquility, prosperity, perfectness, fullness, rest, harmony, and the absence of agitation or discord. William J. Morford, author/translator of *The One New Man Bible*, defines *shalom* in this way:

> Shalom cannot be translated into English with a single word. Shalom comes from Shalem meaning to be complete. When there is Shalom, there is tranquility, justice, sufficient food, clothing, housing. There is Divine health, with no sickness. Shalom means an absence of: disorder, injustice, bribery, corruption, conflict, lack, hatred, abuse, violence, pain, suffering, immorality, and all other negative forces.[2]

*Shalom* **means the absence of negative forces.**

Why would health and healing be included in peace? Peace brings us into alignment with the kingdom of God. We are commanded to let *"the peace of God rule"* in our heart (Col. 3:15). God sets everything in order when He rules. When we are healthy, our body is functioning harmoniously. Everything is in order. All systems are working together properly and our cells are healthy. Often, as soon as emotional barriers are removed, healing manifests.

There is much more to biblical peace than serenity or absence of turmoil. Peace is the power that establishes the government of the Prince of Peace—in all areas of life.

> *For to us a Child is born, to us a Son is given; and the government shall be upon His shoulder, and His name shall be called Wonderful Counselor, Mighty God, Everlasting Father [of Eternity],* **Prince of Peace.** *Of the increase of His government and of peace there shall be no end* (Isaiah 9:6-7 AMP).

The phrase "Prince of Peace," *Sar Shalom* in Hebrew, takes on a far richer meaning when we understand the power of peace. As Prince of Peace, Jesus is the King and Absolute Ruler of the universe. He spoke, "Peace!" into chaos at the time of creation and the order was established. Jesus is the One *still* commanding, "Peace, be still," to the storms of life (see Mark 4:39). When this King occupies a territory, He takes charge. His government is established and His peace brings harmony, or alignment with God.

> *J*esus still commands, "Peace, be still," to the storms of life.

## Peace Guides

Peace provides an amazing key for receiving guidance from the Lord. When we are unsure about what direction to take, we must first become neutral about our options. In other words, we must let go of our preferences and be comfortable letting God decide. Then, in an attitude of prayer, present each possibility before the Lord one at a time. Peace indicates "yes," while an uncomfortable feeling means "no." Occasionally, we may not feel discomfort per se, but notice that the presence of God increases more on one option than the other. That is also a "yes."

> *Let the peace (soul harmony which comes) from Christ rule (act as umpire continually) in your hearts [deciding and settling with finality all questions that arise in your minds]...* (Colossians 3:15 AMP)

### Peace Guards

Peace is spiritual armor: *"The peace of God, which surpasses all understanding, will guard your hearts and minds through Christ Jesus"* (Phil. 4:7). The enemy can't touch the fruit of the Spirit. Peace is a way of life. We are told to walk in shoes of peace (see Eph. 6:15). Peace is militant power that triumphs over the enemy: *"The God of peace will crush Satan under your feet"* (Rom. 16:20).

### The Molecule of Peace

The neuropeptide serotonin is called the "molecule of happiness." Happiness consists of pleasure and contentment. The spiritual counterpart to serotonin is the *peace of God*. Although serotonin is good, supernatural peace has a much more powerful impact on the physical body than natural serotonin.

Jesus never withdraws the gift of peace He has given us, so it is always available to draw on in time of need. When His peace rules our heart, we know Jesus is ruling in our life at that moment. Jesus said, *"Peace I leave with you, My peace I give to you; not as the world gives do I give to you. Let not your heart be troubled, neither let it be afraid"* (John 14:27).

If we happen to lose our peace temporarily, how do we return to peace? Forgiveness! Forgiveness always gets us right back into the atmosphere of the kingdom of God (see Col. 1:13). When you got saved, did you have to wait to receive God's forgiveness? No, it happened instantly. Forgiveness is always available and forgiveness never fails.

*A*llow God to transform negative emotions into His emotions.

We should let our emotions become cherished *friends* that confirm the presence of peace or alert us to negative emotions. Once we know a toxic emotion is present, we can make a *supernatural exchange*. We can then present our negative emotions to God and allow Him to *transform* them into His emotions.

We have a daily choice to either live the abundant life with the supernatural peace Jesus promised us or live under the influence of the law of sin and death (see Rom. 8:2). As God said in Deuteronomy 30:19, *"Choose life."*

> *The thief comes only to steal and kill and destroy; I came that they may have life, and have it abundantly* (John 10:10 NASB).

"*C*hoose life!"

# ENDNOTES

1. D. Clark and J. Clark, *The Supernatural Power of Peace*, (Shippensburg, PA: Destiny Image Publishers, Inc., 2015), 181.

2. W.J. Morford, *The One New Man Bible*, (Traveler's Rest, SC: True Potential Publishing, Inc., 2011), 1780.

*Chapter 9*

# THE PROCESS TOWARD HEALTH
By Dr. Jen

From the time Dennis and I married, my health has continuously improved ever since I began to deal with buried toxic emotions through forgiveness. In the process of allowing God to heal my heart of hidden toxic emotions, physical healing has been a concurrent blessing that often springs forth automatically. If I become aware of a need for healing, I ask the Lord to reveal contributing emotional issues. God has been faithful to give me the answers I need in prayer.

God is so much smarter than we are. He knit us together in our mother's womb and He knows the location of all the "tangles" adversely affecting our health.

*You created my inmost being; You knit me together in my mother's womb. I praise You because I am fearfully and wonderfully made; Your works are wonderful, I*

*know that full well. My frame was not hidden from*
*You when I was made in the secret place* (Psalm
139:13-15 NIV).

### Surprised by Healing

As God deals with issues in our heart, He often touches
our body in ways that surprise us. In every one of the following cases, physical healing was a side benefit of emotional
healing. Because 90 percent of physical disease is emotionally
based, we always encourage people who need physical healing
to start praying through emotional issues. Sometimes only one
emotional wounding precipitated an illness, but there could be
several involved.

### Color Blindness Healed

Once, when Dennis and I (Jen) were ministering at a church
in New England, we had an altar call for those who needed to
forgive. Ben came up for prayer to forgive his father. Much to
his amazement, he was instantly healed of color blindness as
soon as he forgave. Because Ben was an artist, this was a double
blessing for him. He told us later that he almost drove off the
road the first time he saw a sunset! Only God knew what had
caused Ben's color blindness. When the barrier was removed,
healing occurred automatically.

### A Heart Healed

I (Jen) received forgiveness for taking in fear and experienced instant deliverance and physical healing.

A month or two after Dennis and I were married
in 1997, I was jerked awake out of a sound sleep

by a rapidly racing and pounding heartbeat and a cold sweat. I knew exactly what was happening: paroxysmal atrial tachycardia (PAT). This consists of extremely rapid heartbeats for a period that begins and ends abruptly. The heart rate suddenly shoots upward to 140–220 beats a minute and it feels like it simply won't slow down.

My heart was beating so fast that it felt like the bed was shaking. This was not a new thing, but a symptom that had tormented me several times a month for the past 20 years. Dennis awakened and felt my fear flooding the room. I felt fear in my gut and also surrounding me. Fortunately, he helped me pray through this, and I felt the fear leave instantly. I received forgiveness and instantly fear was replaced by peace inside me and the fear in the room left. My heart immediately stopped palpitating and returned to a gentle, normal rhythm. The atrial tachycardia never occurred again.[1]

Dennis and I didn't pray for healing; we just removed the fear, and deliverance and healing happened automatically.

### Irritable Bowel Syndrome Healed

Rob forgave someone who had betrayed him and he was healed of a bowel condition.

After a trusted friend betrayed him, Rob lived with a continual undercurrent of resentment in his heart. Every time he thought about the other person, he got angry. Time and time again, Rob had said, "I forgive him"—but he remained a captive to his anger nevertheless. No matter how hard he tried, he couldn't shake his inner torment. When Rob met with us, Dennis prayed him through emotional healing. In just a few short minutes, years of frustration and anger were replaced by a deep inner peace. The constant emotional gnawing in his gut vanished and, as a bonus, he was instantly healed of irritable bowel syndrome (IBS)![2]

### Allergies Healed

Dennis's son, Jason, moved to Fort Mill, South Carolina, from Kansas to become part of our ministry. He testifies that numerous healings have spontaneously occurred since he has been allowing God to heal issues from his past. He didn't pray for healing; healing was automatic when he dealt with suppressed emotions. Jason says:

> I have been healed of all sorts of food allergies including all tree nuts, apples, pears, grapes, and water chestnuts. When I ate any of these, my mouth would feel itchy and my throat would swell up. Sometimes I also experienced stomach pain. Now I can eat anything I want with no problem.
>
> I was also allergic to many cleaning products, detergents, and Styrofoam. Grass, especially newly cut, would cause my eyes to become red and watering and my nose would start running. If I slept on a feather pillow or sat on sofa cushions filled

with feathers my sinuses would clog and I would develop a sore throat. All these allergies are gone.

I suffered from allergies to dogs and cats (it was worse with dogs). I couldn't comfortably be in a room where cats had been or even hug someone who owned a cat. My eyes would get red, my nose would run, and I would break out in hives. I have been healed of all my allergies just by letting God deal with emotional issues in my past.

### *Allergy Healed*

I forgave my grandmother and was instantly healed of an allergy to chicken. —Karl, Connecticut

### *One-Hundred-Pound Weight Loss Following Emotional Healing*

I forgave my mother and instantly felt relief from emotional pain. I had become very overweight due to emotional eating. Over the next six months, the weight just came off. I lost one hundred pounds. I didn't even have to buy new clothes because the Lord supernaturally prompted people to give me all the clothes I needed. He gave me a brand-new wardrobe. —Sarah, Virginia

### *Tumor Disappeared*

Sandra had participated in a number of our training sessions and was very excited to share this testimony. During a mission trip to Africa, she had the opportunity to pray with a woman who had been traumatized as a child. When she led her through prayer for forgiveness, the woman's emotional pain and fear were healed instantly. Moreover, when Sandra saw her again the next day, she joyfully testified that a grapefruit-sized tumor in her abdomen had simply vanished.

### Emotions and Health

In recent years, the scientific community has dramatically increased its attention to the relationship between emotions and health. Strong connections have been made between the central nervous system and the immune system, which were once thought to be completely independent systems. Studies now demonstrate that *emotional states affect physical states* in profound ways.

> No one can really be well without dealing with their emotional health. This may seem like a radical idea, but for so many people with intractable health problems, there won't be any progress on a physical level—no matter what therapy is used—until there is progress at the emotional level. "The body never lies"—even if the emotional problem developed 50 years ago.[3]

Researchers from Carnegie Mellon University and the University of British Columbia found that emotional distress is connected to stress, depression, cardiovascular disease, and depressed immune system function.[4] Other studies demonstrate that *suppressing* negative emotions adversely affects health.[5] Emotions don't die; we just bury them alive.

---

*E*motions don't die; we just bury them alive.

---

A long-term study undertaken by leading medical research-ers strongly indicates that chronic anger and hostility can cause premature death. Those individuals scoring in the "high range on hostility scales are almost five times more likely to die of heart disease than those scoring lower. They were also seven times more likely to die by age fifty."[6]

What does this mean for us? If we retain negative emo-tional information in our cells, it has detrimental effects on our health. It is clear that, over the course of a lifetime, the toxic emotions stored in our cells from childhood cause the illnesses of adulthood. Buried negative emotions also become barriers that *block* our healing even when we yield to the Divine Healer. However, if we cleanse toxic emotions from our cells, it is logical to suppose that our health will improve—automatically. When God heals our emotions, the Holy Spirit is free to heal our body—even changing the iden-tity and health of our cells.

> *W*hen God heals our emotions, the
> Holy Spirit is free to heal our body.

Our immune system does not exist in isolation from daily experience.... When [toxic] emotions are repressed...this inhibition disarms the body's defences against illness. Repression—dissociating emotions from awareness and relegating them to the unconscious realm—disorganizes and con-fuses our physiological defences so that in some people these defences go awry, becoming the destroyers of health rather than its protectors.[7]

### Removing Barriers

Toxic emotions are not only harmful to the body but can actually *block* healing until removed. Therefore, when we seek healing, we may need to persevere as God untangles the emotional underpinnings of certain conditions. However, it is quite common for just one emotional healing to result in a physical healing.

When we learn to deal with toxic emotions, thus removing barriers to healing in us, physical healing can simply manifest. Dennis and I (Jen) have experienced many "accidental" physical healings without ever praying specifically for healing by just dealing regularly with negative emotions. We may not know the precipitating cause of an ailment, but God certainly does. If we have a specific symptom, the first thing we do is ask the Lord to show us any underlying emotional issues and pray them through. As soon as we do that, physical healing usually manifests without further prayer.

*Toxic emotions can block healing.*

### Four Diseases Healed

I was diagnosed by my doctor with four serious diseases after some lab results came back. I prayed through every emotional issue the Lord showed me and began yielding to the Divine Healer in me.

I was supernaturally healed of all four conditions. The next time I had lab work done, all the tests came back negative. My doctor was astounded. I now had no symptoms plus medical evidence of healing. —Debra, South Carolina

## Cancer Healed

I had been diagnosed with terminal cancer. After learning that negative emotions can make us prone to disease, I prayed through every emotional issue the Lord showed me. Now I am in complete remission and there is no evidence of any cancer in my body. —Sondra, New York

## Swollen Joints Healed

I could hardly use my hands the joints were so swollen and painful. I started forgiving whoever the Lord brought to my mind. Then, I welcomed Christ the healer into my entire body. The swelling and pain went away completely. —Audree, Massachusetts

## Removing Barriers to Health

As we can see, the answer to the question, "Are emotions important to our health?" is *"Yes!"* Research shows that emotions have great power over the physical body. Emotions create the conditions for health or sickness. Approximately 90 percent of all diseases are emotionally based.

It has also been estimated that even the best healing evangelists have only a ten percent success rate. If believers simply dealt with their own *emotional barriers* to healing, it is logical to assume that the numbers of those healed would increase dramatically.

A study conducted at the University of Kansas shows that emotions profoundly affect physical health.

> A researcher from the University of Kansas has spearheaded a new investigation into the link between emotions and health. The research proves that positive emotions are critical for upkeep of physical health for people worldwide.... Data from the Gallup World Poll drove the findings, with adults in more than 140 countries.... Even without shelter or food, positive emotions were shown to boost health."[8]

*E*motions create the conditions
for health or sickness.

A long-term study undertaken by leading medical researchers strongly indicates that chronic anger and hostility can cause premature death. Those individuals scoring in the "high range on hostility scales are almost five times more likely to die of heart disease than those scoring lower. They were also seven times more likely to die by age fifty."[9]

What does this mean for us? If we retain negative emotional information in our cells, it has detrimental effects on our health. Stored negative emotions also become barriers that *block* our healing even when we yield to the Divine Healer. However, if we cleanse toxic emotions from our cells, it is logical to suppose that our health will improve—automatically. When God heals our emotions, the Holy Spirit is free to heal our body—even changing the identity and health of our cells.

When God rules our thoughts, choices, and emotions, we feel peace. When God rules our body, we experience health. As the soul—the mind, will, and emotions—is filled more and more with the Holy Spirit, the Lord releases health to the body. This is the process of "sanctification." In simple terms, sanctification is the means by which God increases the rule of His kingdom in our lives.

> *W*hen God rules, we feel peace
> and experience health.

Legally, because of what Christ accomplished on the cross of Calvary—the reconciliation of God and man—we have received *full provision* for healing and health.[10] The psalmist declares that God is the One *"who forgives all your iniquities, who heals all your diseases"* (Ps. 103:3). And Peter reminds us that *"His divine power has given to us all things that pertain to life and godliness"* (2 Pet. 1:3).

We were given access to the blessing of healing at Calvary, but we need to *believe in the finished work of Christ* and *remove barriers in us* to experience the reality of this divine health. If our thoughts are still riddled with the lies of the enemy and our feelings poisoned by negative emotions, however subtle they may be, our body will continue to be vulnerable to sickness.

We can *limit* God by *failing to appropriate* all that has been provided in our spiritual inheritance or by *failing to allow Him to remove the barriers* in our own hearts. The psalmist tells of the children of Israel doing this very thing:

> *Their heart was not steadfast with Him, nor were they faithful in His covenant.... Yes, again and again they tempted God, and limited the Holy One of Israel* (Psalm 78:37,41).

*W*e limit God by failing to remove the barriers in our own hearts.

### *The Conscious Mind and Non-Conscious Mind*

In Romans 12:2, we are told to renew our minds. However, the word for "mind" in the original Greek is *nous*, referring to thought, emotions, and will. So *mind*, then, is our whole being, which includes our heart, not just our thoughts. The word *mind* in the Bible is more appropriately termed "mindset" in keeping with Hebrew thought. This sheds new light on the words of Paul:

> *Do not be conformed to this world, but be transformed by the renewing of your mind, that you may prove what is that good and acceptable and perfect will of God* (Romans 12:2).

Our conscious mind is active and creative—it plans out the future, remembers the past, and lives in the present. Our consciousness is a tiny speck compared to the vast galaxy of our non-conscious self. Researchers estimate that our conscious mind can process only about 2,000 bits of information per second while our non-conscious mind can process 400 billion bits. Neural impulses in our non-conscious mind travel at a rate almost 800 times that of the neural impulses of our conscious mind.

The vast amount of data in our non-conscious mind includes input from our five senses, perceptions, self-talk, memories, and beliefs. All this information is filtered through our Reticular Activating System (RAS), located in the brain stem, to form our conscious understanding based on internal filters.

Scripture suggests the presence of an "unknown" aspect of our heart and mind:

> *Who can discern his lapses and errors? Clear me from hidden [and unconscious] faults. Keep back Your servant also from presumptuous sins; let them not have dominion over me! Then shall I be blameless, and I shall be innocent and clear of great transgression* (Psalm 19:12-13 AMP).

*We* only *think* we know ourselves.

The non-conscious lives only in the present tense based on what has been learned in the past including memories, impressions, wounds and angers, truth and lies. These lessons are stronger than willpower. The non-conscious is much more powerful than the force of our human will. We live our lives out of the perceptions from the *combined* conscious and non-conscious parts of our being—our *heart*. What can account for the Romans 7 experience? "I don't do what I want to do, but the things I don't want to do, those things I do!" That is our non-conscious at work!

> *For what I am doing, I do not understand. For what I will to do, that I do not practice; but what I hate, that I do* (Romans 7:15).

---

> *T*he non-conscious is much more
> powerful than willpower.

---

In times of crisis many individuals have been surprised by their actions, both good and bad. We only *think* we know ourselves. In truth, we don't fully know our *own* heart, and others know us only by what they observe and experience. God is the only One who knows us in our entirety.

> *The heart is deceitful above all things...who can know it?* (Jeremiah 17:9)

The "Johari Window," named after the first names of its inventors, Joseph Luft and Harry Ingham, is a tool for understanding ourselves. A "window" with four panes divides our personal awareness into four levels: open, hidden, blind, and unknown (see the following table).

|  | KNOWN TO SELF | NOT KNOWN TO SELF |
|---|---|---|
| **KNOWN TO OTHERS** | 1 Open | 2 Blind Spots |
| **NOT KNOWN TO OTHERS** | 3 Hidden | 4 Unknown |

As we can see in the upper left quadrant, there is a part of us that is *open*. We know these things about ourselves and other people observe these same things. In the bottom left quadrant, there is the part of us that we know about but keep *hidden* from others. There are also parts of us that others know but to which we are blind, as we see in the upper right quadrant. These are our "blind spots." And there is also an area that is unknown to everyone, including ourselves. God Himself is the only One who knows that quadrant of our soul. Our non-conscious mind falls in this "unknown" category. How do we begin to access the areas in which we are blind to ourselves, or the areas that are completely unknown to us and others? Only God knows how to cleanse our heart.

*As the soul is sanctified, the new creation is revealed.*

David offers us an excellent example of how to seek the Lord's help for healing our heart. David allowed God to have full access to his heart. Psalm 19 illustrates David's process of approaching the Lord for cleansing and deliverance. David admitted to God that the *unknown things lodged in his heart* could lead to very serious consequences.

> *Who can understand his errors? Cleanse me from secret faults. Keep back Your servant also from presumptuous sins; let them not have dominion over me. Then I shall be blameless, and I shall be innocent of great transgression. Let the words of my mouth and the meditation of my heart be acceptable in Your sight, O Lord, my strength and my Redeemer* (Psalm 19:12-14).

### Jesus Is the Forgiver

Jesus in us does the forgiving through us. Through grace we are saved, and by grace we live in the Spirit. It is no longer I who live, but Christ who lives in me. Therefore, it is no longer I who love, but Christ who loves in me. It is no longer I who forgive, but Christ who forgives in me! *"My old self has been crucified with Christ. It is no longer I who live, but Christ lives in me. So I live in this earthly body by trusting in the Son of God, who loved me and gave Himself for me"* (Gal. 2:20 NLT).

Christ the forgiver in us does all the work. And everything He does is easy for Him! All we have to do is yield and allow Him to do the work. *"It is God who works in you both to will and to do for His good pleasure"* (Phil. 2:13). What do *we* do then? We yield our will to God's will and He does the work.

### Important Keys for Prayer

Forgiveness is the answer for dealing with conflict and offenses in the moment as well as the baggage of the past. Christ is the Forgiver, so forgiveness works every time! It is instant, not a process, just like when you got saved. Deal with whatever God shows you, even if you think it is unimportant. There is no "big or little." If you think it is too traumatic to face, you only have to feel a bit of the pain momentarily to present it to Jesus for healing. It's all easy for Jesus! Finally, sequence is important, so always go in God's order. Pray through one thing at a time until you get peace.

### *Forgive in Three Directions*

Forgiveness goes in three directions—toward God, self, and others. Sometimes we must forgive in two or more directions. If in doubt, forgive. You can't love or forgive too much!

1. *God.* God didn't do anything wrong, but people get angry at Him anyway. Sometimes people feel hurt that God didn't do what they wanted Him to do, or become angry that God didn't *stop* something from happening. Forgiving God gets *your* heart right by releasing your judgments toward Him.

2. *Self.* If you are angry, disappointed with, or ashamed of yourself, you need to receive forgiveness for judging yourself so harshly. Frequently people are much harder on themselves than other people!

3. *Others.* Release forgiveness to other people. It sets you free!

### *Steps of Forgiveness*

When praying about physical healing, ask God to show you the entry points of negative emotions contributing to your physical condition. Toxic emotions are barriers to healing. There may be just one entry point or an *emotional cluster* of several negative emotions.

- *Pray.* Close your eyes and pray. Put your hand on your belly and yield to Christ within. As soon as you yield, you feel the peace of God's presence.

  - If you are angry at God, start by forgiving Him.

- *First.* What is the first person or situation that comes to mind—in an image or specific memory? (We want a real person or real situation, not prophetic imagery.)

- *Feel.* Feel the emotion attached to that person or situation. Every thought has a corresponding emotion. *Allow* yourself to feel. What is the emotion you feel in your gut?

- *Forgive.* Yield to Christ the forgiver within and allow a river of forgiveness to flow toward God or others, or receive it for yourself. You don't have to try; just relax and let Him do the work.

Most of the time, we just need the three steps of First-Feel-Forgive. In approximately one out of 30 or 40 emotional woundings, a repetitive negative thought is connected, such as, "I don't belong," "I'm a failure," or "I'll always be alone." Assess the thought. Is it something God would say? Does it have the love of God attached to it? If not, don't receive it. Remember, if God didn't give it to you, you don't want it. If there *is* a repetitive thought, deal with the emotion first and get peace. Then go on to the following step. (A *fact* is what God says is true.)

- **Fact.** After forgiving and getting peace, if there is a negative thought of a lie, renounce the lie out loud. Next, ask the Lord for the truth (scriptural fact) and receive it. Truth rises up from your spirit and informs your mind.

## PRACTICE

### REMOVE BARRIERS: PRAYER STEP 4

Negative emotions are barriers to healing. If you are angry at God, start by forgiving Him.

*First-Feel-Forgive*

- *Pray.* Close your eyes and pray, placing your hand on your belly.
- *Inquire.* Ask, "Where did this get started in my life?"
- *First.* Focus on the first person or situation that comes to mind.
- *Feel.* Allow yourself to feel the negative emotion momentarily.
- *Forgive.* Yield to Christ the forgiver within. Allow a river of forgiveness to flow toward God or others, or receive it for yourself until you feel peace.

## TROUBLESHOOTING

### FILLING EMOTIONAL NEEDS

After forgiving and replacing lies (if there are any) with the truth of God, let God fill emotional needs that weren't met.

- *Fill.* If you have an emotional need that wasn't met (for example, love or approval), forgive the person(s) who should have met that need but didn't.
  - Release them into the hands of God until you no longer feel an inner demand concerning them.
  - When you have peace, welcome God into that area to fill the need.

# ENDNOTES

1. D. Clark and J. Clark, *Deep Relief Now: Healed, Free, Whole*, (Shippensburg, PA: Destiny Image Publishers, Inc., 2014), 157.

2. Ibid., 141.

3. M. Pick, "How Emotional Experience Determines Your Health," *Women to Women* (2006). Retrieved July 9, 2007 from http://www.womentowomen.com/emotions-anxiety-mood/how-emotional-experience-determines-your-health.

4. D. Cohen, D. Janicki-Deverts, and G. Miller, "Psychological Stress and Disease," *Journal of the American Medical Association (JAMA)* 298, no. 14 (2007), 1,685–1,687.

5. J. Gross and R. Levenson, "Hiding Feelings: The Acute Effects of Inhibiting Positive and Negative Emotions," *Journal of Abnormal Psychology* 106 (1997), 95–103.

6. J. Pennebaker, "Inhibition as the Linchpin of Health," qtd. in H.S. Freidman (Editor), *Hostility, Coping, and Health*, (Washington, D.C.: American Psychological Association, 1992), 127–139.

7. G. Maté, *When the Body Says No: Exploring the Stress-Disease Connection* (Hoboken, NJ: John Wiley & Sons, Inc., 2011), 7.

8. S. Pressman, "University of Kansas Research Finds Human Emotions Hold Sway over Physical Health Worldwide," *Psychology and Sociology* (March 4, 2009). Retrieved November 29, 2010 from http://esciencenews.com/articles/2009/03/04/university.kansas.research.finds.human.emotions.hold.sway.over.physical.health.worldwide.

9. J. Barefoot, et al., "Hostility CHD Incidence in Total Mortality—A Twenty-Five Year Follow-Up Study of Twenty-Five Physicians," *Psychosomatic Medicine* 45 (1984), 79-83.

10. The atonement of Christ is the sacrificial work of Jesus on behalf of sinners. In His death on the cross, Christ atoned for the sins of humanity so that God was satisfied, and reconciliation was available for those who believe. The ground of redemption for fallen humanity is the obedience and death of a Savior. *"While we were yet sinners, Christ died for us"* (Rom. 5:8 KJV). Because of forgiveness, we have access to God. The atonement paid the price for the redemption of the whole man—spirit, soul, and body (including physical healing and ultimate glorification).

# Chapter 10

# CONTROL ABOVE GENETICS

Can what we *believe* override our genetics? The answer to that question is a most emphatic, *"Yes!"* Consider the remarkable case of a young doctor named Albert Mason and a boy with a terminal condition. In 1952, Dr. Mason began treating a 15-year old boy with what appeared to be a bad case of warts.[1]

No conventional medical treatment had been able to help him. Twice doctors tried skin grafts, but his new skin soon flared up with the same condition. The boy was referred to Dr. Mason. In other cases, Dr. Mason had successfully used the power of belief to remove warts, so he scheduled a session for the boy.

> When the boy came back a week later, Mason was gratified to see that the arm looked healthy. But when Mason brought the boy to the referring surgeon, who had unsuccessfully tried to help the

boy with skin grafts, he learned that he had made
a medical error.[2]

The surgeon was astonished when he saw the appearance of
the boy's arm. It turned out that the boy did not just have warts
but a potentially deadly genetic condition called congenital ich-
thyosis. The boy had reversed his symptoms by *believing*.

It was clear that something astonishing had occurred. The
change was not due to medical treatment. The reason behind
this great success was not due to a change in thinking. The key
element was the power of *belief*. What we believe can override
our genetics. The afflicted boy had apparently become convinced in his heart that he was healed.

*What* **we believe can override our genetics.**

### The Fallacy of Genetic Determinism

In 1910, scientists discovered hereditary information in
cells. In 1953, James Watson, American molecular biologist,
geneticist, and zoologist, and Francis Crick, British molecular
biologist, biophysicist, and neuroscientist, discovered the structure of DNA (deoxyribonucleic acid) and the fact that DNA
replicates itself.

Based on their research, scientists made an assumption:
DNA controls its own replication and is its own "boss."[3] However, the idea that genes control our biology has been greatly
challenged by the latest scientific research. Contrary to what is

commonly believed in the world today, DNA is not our destiny. The glory of God is our destiny.

Research has demonstrated that environmental factors are more powerful than genetics in determining the characteristics of organisms. A new field of biology, *epigenetics*, studies changes in gene activity based on manipulations of the environment. The word *epigenetics* means "control above genetics". Epigenetics proposes that genetics can be *controlled* by environmental influences such as nutrition, stress, and emotions. These influences can actually *modify how genes are expressed* without changing the basic blueprint.[3]

---

*D*NA is not our destiny.

---

A groundbreaking experiment in epigenetics was conducted at Duke University in 2000. Randy Jirtle, professor of radiation oncology at Duke University, and Robert Waterland, a postdoctoral student, designed a simple but groundbreaking experiment. They started with pairs of *agouti mice* that carried a particular gene—the Agouti gene. This gene caused the mice and their offspring to have yellow coats and ravenous appetites, which led to gross obesity and often premature death. Additionally, the mice were prone to developing certain cancers and diabetes. When agouti mice breed, almost all the offspring share the same traits as the parents.

The researchers modified the environment of a group of parent mice by feeding them a diet rich in *methyl donors*.[4] These small chemical clusters are able to attach to a gene and "turn it off." Unlike their parents, the agouti mice offspring were slim with brown coats. They were also not susceptible to the same cancers and diabetes as their parents and lived to an energetic old age.

Manipulation of the diet had completely suppressed the effects of the Agouti gene. Even more significant was the finding that the gene suppression was passed on to succeeding generations even though they still carried the same gene.[5] The change was astounding! By altering the diet of the mice, Jirtle and Waterland had demonstrated that epigenetic signals from the environment can be passed on to the subsequent generations without changing a single gene sequence.

If DNA is *not* in control, then how are genes "activated"? As the agouti mice experiment demonstrated, genes are "turned on" by signals from the environment. Without an environmental signal, the genes will remain dormant. Some environmental signals that activate or suppress genes are *nutrients, stress,* and *emotions* (both positive and negative).

*O*ur genes are activated by our environment.

Most people have genes that should allow them to live healthy lives. Only two percent of diseases are the result of a single gene; most diseases arise from multiple genes *and* their interaction with the environment.

> Epigenetic modifications are central to many human diseases, including cancer. Traditionally, cancer has been viewed as a genetic disease, and it is now becoming apparent that the onset of cancer is preceded by epigenetic abnormalities.[6]

This *combination* of "nature and nurture" is the precipitating factor in many diseases, including cancer, heart disease, and diabetes. Only five percent of cancers and heart disease, in fact, are due to heredity. As it turns out, almost all—95 percent—of cancers are triggered by *factors other than genetics.*

*A*lmost all cancers are caused by factors other than genetics.

### The Smart Cell

How does the environment impact cells in such a dramatic fashion? To answer that question, we must understand some facts about cellular biology. Human beings are "communities" of approximately 50 to 75 trillion cells. Each of these cells could survive on its own if isolated and placed in a Petri dish. The interior of the cell contains small organs, or "organelles," that perform a variety of tasks necessary to sustain life.

## Cell Structure

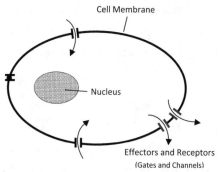

The cell interior has a nucleus containing genetic information (DNA) in addition to various organelles, such as the Golgi apparatus and mitochondria, which makes up the working "factory" system of cellular life.

Remarkably, each cell functions with *purposeful intent*, thus exhibiting individual *intelligence*. For example, cells avoid environments that are unpleasant and are attracted to environments beneficial to growth. Moreover, they are able to *learn* through their environmental experiences, forming *cellular memories,* such as antibodies for disease, that are transmitted to their offspring in cell division.

It was once believed that the "nucleus" was the brain of the cell. Scientists now understand that the nucleus simply contains the cell's genetic information. What *is* the brain of the cell? A brain is the director of all processes in an organism. It receives information then directs responses accordingly. This is exactly what the cell membrane does. *The actual brain of the cell is the cell membrane.*

The nucleus of the cell, therefore, is not the brain but the *reproductive system* of the cell. Because the nucleus is responsible for the cell's reproductive capacity, it functions as the "gonad" of the cell. The nucleus replicates itself in cell division to form offspring, and it reproduces proteins necessary for the cell to function and remain healthy.

The cell membrane has *receptors* that are constantly aware of the environment and respond according to environmental information. When the environment communicates with a cell membrane, the "brain" of the cell determines what the *response* of the cell will be. Nothing can enter or exit the cell membrane without being monitored by cellular intelligence. Changes in the interior of the cell are also orchestrated by the cell membrane.

### *Belief Controls Genetics*

Cells are created by God to live and thrive when their environment is healthy. Recent discoveries in cellular biology bridge *science and spirit*. Because cells have an inherent capacity to maintain health when their environment is healthy, we should first scrutinize the environment of the cells, *spiritual* as well as physical, when any *lack* of health is present.

The various receptors on the cell membrane respond to different kinds of signals—some responding to signals within the cell, some responding to environmental signals such as nutrients, and others responding *only* to vibrational energy fields or spiritual "energy."[7] *Energy* receptors "vibrate" like tuning forks and modify their shape based on the influences of the environment. The cell then responds based on the information received.

How does the cell membrane react to its environmental influences and affect our DNA? Our cells contain special proteins on their individual DNA strands. The DNA itself (our chromosomes) makes up the central core of the gene. The proteins that cover the DNA function like a *protective sleeve*. Environmental signals transmitted by the cell membrane change the shape of the sleeve to *activate* or *suppress* genetic information. As we have seen, belief has power to suppress genes. If scientists now know that environment controls DNA, then how much more is *God* in control of genetics?

As discussed earlier, energy receptors can "read" energy fields. Energy signals are transmitted by various forms of energy including belief and prayer. What we believe in our heart can change our biology. Belief "energy"—thoughts, attitudes, and emotions—can activate or inhibit cellular functioning in either constructive or destructive ways.

> *T*he power of *believing prayer* has
> tremendous influence on our body.

The power of *believing prayer* has tremendous influence on the cells, organs, and systems of our body. Prayer is not just talking, although it can include talking. Prayer is, first of all, being with a Person. True prayer is a spiritual encounter.

When we pray, we come to Jesus and make a spirit-to-Spirit connection with Him. Jesus admonished the Pharisees for failing to come to Him, saying: *"You search the Scriptures, for in them you think you have eternal life; and these are they which testify of Me. But you are not willing to come to Me that you may have life"* (John 5:39-40). When we yield to the Lord, we touch His presence.

Every time we touch the presence of God, we are changed. When we add spoken words or pray silent prayers, we have already tapped into the healing power of God. It is impossible to spend even a short while in prayer without affecting our body in a positive way.

> *E*very time we touch the presence
> of God, we are changed.

However, at times we must actively pursue God to prevail in prayer. Consider this verse of Scripture: *"The effective, fervent prayer of a righteous man avails much"* (James 5:16). "Effective," *energēs* in the Greek, means "active" and "full of power". Great power is released when an individual becomes aligned with God. The Greek word for "fervent," *ektenēs,* means "earnestly," "assiduously," and "without ceasing". "Avail," *ischuo* in the Greek, means "to be strong," "to be in sound health," or "to wield power". So what is produced by this effective, earnest prayer? "Energy" for healing is released from our heart through Christ the healer within. Prayer has the spiritual force to produce strength and health. Prayer changes things, including our physical health. *"Whatever things you ask when you pray, believe that you receive them, and you will have them"* (Mark 11:24).

What we believe in our heart can change our biology. When we yield to God, we tap into His healing power.

> *W*hat we believe in our heart can change our biology.

## ENDNOTES

1. A.A. Mason, "A case of congenital ichthyosiform erythrodermia of Brocq," *British Medical Journal* 30 (1952), 441–443. The power of belief can produce results even if the diagnosis is wrong or the treatment is unorthodox, alternative, or a placebo.

2. Lipton, *The Biology of Belief*, 123-124.

3. Ibid., 153; L.A. Pray, "Epigenetics: Genome, Meet Your Environment," *The Scientist* 18, no. 13 (July 5, 2004), 14–20.

4. Methyl donors are found in many foods, including soy beans, garlic, onions, and beets.

5. R.L. Jirtle and R.A. Waterland, "Transposable elements: targets for early nutritional effects on epigenetic gene regulation," *Molecular Cell Biology* Should read "23, no. 5 (2003), 293-300.

6. R. Kanwal and S. Gupta, "Epigenetics and Cancer," *Journal of Applied Physiology* 109, no. 2 (August 2010), 598–605.

7. Lipton, *The Biology of Belief*, 84.

# INTERLUDE

*Had I a mind to hinder the progress of the gospel, and to establish the kingdom of darkness, I would go about, telling people they might have the Spirit of God, and yet not feel it.*
—GEORGE WHITEFIELD

George Whitefield (1714–1770), Anglican cleric and evangelist from Great Britain, was instrumental in spreading the First Great Awakening in England and, especially, in the American colonies. He is one of the most famous religious figures in American history. Whitefield preached on two continents, reaching perhaps ten million hearers in his lifetime. His listeners were awestruck by the sheer power of his oratory. It is said that virtually every man, woman, and child in the colonies had heard him preach at least once. Newspapers called Whitefield the "marvel of the age" and the "Grand Itinerant."

Because he delivered a common salvation message of Jesus above all, Whitefield was able to cut across cultural, denominational, and state lines to make America truly *one nation under God* for the first time.[1] Whitefield, however, found himself viciously maligned, not by secularists, but by Christian *clergymen*. The ensuing firestorm split the church world into two camps—head versus heart Christianity. It is said that the controversy was responsible for quenching the work of God and greatly limiting the move of the Holy Spirit.

With characteristic boldness and courage, Whitefield waded right into the tempest and confronted the opposition by delivering his famous Sermon 38, "The Indwelling of the Spirit, the Common Privilege of All Believers." In it, Whitefield declared that Christians have been given great promises by God—to be partakers of the divine nature, to have spiritual union with Jesus, and to know Christ with us (see John 17:20-22), thus intimately knowing and experiencing God (see 1 John 1:1-3). Consider Whitefield's rebuttal in his own words:

> St. Peter tells us, "we have many great and precious promises, that we may be made partakers of the divine nature;" our Lord prays, "that we may be one, as the Father and He are one;" and our own church, in conformity to these texts of Scripture, in her excellent communion-office, tells us, that those who receive the sacrament worthily, "dwell in Christ, and Christ in them; that they are one with Christ, and Christ with them." And yet,

Christians must have their names cast out as evil, and ministers in particular, must be looked upon as deceivers of the people, for affirming, that we must be really united to God, by receiving the Holy Ghost. Be astonished, O heavens, at this!

Indeed, I will not say, all our letter-learned preachers deny this doctrine in express words; but however, they do in effect; for they talk professedly against inward feelings, and say, we may have God's Spirit without feeling it, which is in reality to deny the thing itself. And had I a mind to hinder the progress of the gospel, and to establish the kingdom of darkness, I would go about, telling people they might have the Spirit of God, and yet not feel it.[2]

Today, Christians are reviled and ministers in particular are slandered as heretics or called "new age" when they suggest we can hear from God and feel His presence. To really understand the nature of spiritual experience, we must ask if it points to making Jesus Lord of every area of life. If Jesus is Lord of our emotions, shouldn't we feel the fruit of the Spirit as a reality? The love of God is not a philosophy but a reality to be experienced. Perhaps we should question those who have cold hearts and little love for God and their brethren instead. And, even then, our response should be earnest prayer rather than accusation.

*Not everyone who says to Me, "Lord, Lord," shall enter the kingdom of heaven, but he who does the will of My Father in heaven. Many will say to Me in that day, "Lord, Lord, have we not prophesied in Your name, cast out demons in Your name, and done many wonders in Your name?" And then I will declare to them, "I never knew you; depart from Me, you who practice lawlessness!"* (Matthew 7:21-23)

Many Christians know Jesus as their Savior but continue to live mostly for themselves. They pose little, if any, threat to the enemy. However, the devil greatly fears those believers who completely surrender to Jesus, thereby truly making Him Lord. The Scriptures clearly reveal that nobody can say, "Jesus is Lord," except by the Holy Spirit. And no evil spirit would ever want believers to submit more completely to the Lordship of Jesus Christ.

*Therefore I want you to know that no one who is speaking by the Spirit of God says, "Jesus be cursed," and no one can say, "Jesus is Lord," except by the Holy Spirit* (1 Corinthians 12:3 NIV).

When Christians in general, and especially ministers, denounce inward feelings and say we may have God's Spirit without experiencing anything, they are denying the reality of the Holy Spirit and saying all we can know is intellectual philosophy.

Although the head versus heart groups still exist, how could the enemy effectively strategize against believers who have *already* discovered the power of authentic Christianity working within their hearts? What if believers discover that they can experience the presence and anointing of God and know the glory of Christ in them (see Col. 1:27)? What if they learn how to forgive, deal with toxic emotions, and tap into the fruit of the Spirit as a lifestyle? What if believers find out that yielding to the Divine Healer within for healing and health is as easy as encountering the Savior at the time of salvation?

What trick could the enemy possibly use to deplete such an army of triumphant believers of their power? Once believers know the reality of the anointing and the fruit of the Spirit, what could the devil possibly do? What Delilah could shear such a Samson of his power?

If the enemy could keep us stressed out, living in willpower instead of God's power, he would render us largely ineffective for God. We cannot experience the peace and presence of God when we are stressed. If the devil wanted to hinder the advance of the gospel and help establish the kingdom of darkness in our time, he would cause our Christianity to be drained of the true power of God through...*stress.*

> [The enemy] *shall speak pompous words against the Most High, shall persecute* [wear out] *the saints of the Most High* (Daniel 7:25).

—but—

> *The people who know their God shall be strong, and carry out great exploits* (Daniel 11:32).

"*The* people who know their God shall be strong, and carry out great exploits!"

# ENDNOTES

1.   P. Marshall and D. Manuel, *The Light and the Glory*, (Old Tappan, NJ: Fleming H. Revell Company, 1977), 251–253.

2.   G. Whitefield, "The Indwelling of the Spirit, the Common Privilege of All Believers," *The Anglican Library*. Retrieved February 9, 2015 from http://www.anglicanlibrary .org/whitefield/sermons/38.htm.

## Chapter 11

# REST FOR THE STRESSED

## BY DR. JEN

I pulled into the driveway and took some deep breaths. My shoulders felt stiff from gripping the steering wheel so tightly all the way home from work. Closing my eyes, I shook my head a little. What a day! I had to learn a whole new system of evaluation, and I greatly preferred the old familiar way I'd done things for years. It made me tense just thinking about it.

Throwing open the car door, I rushed to find Dennis. We had been married for seven months, but I'd learned so much in that short period of time. I'd learned how to commune with God spirit-to-Spirit, how to deal with my emotional issues, and how to release things into God's hands. But what about stress! How do you get rid of that? Almost everyone I knew seemed to be "stressed" much of the time.

Much to my surprise, Dennis said, "That's not such a big deal about changing your evaluations." My mouth dropped open. I was expecting some sympathy. Instead, Dennis said, "You'll get used to it and you're smart. Everyone else has to learn it, too. The problem is that the circumstances don't warrant the amount of stress you're feeling. There must be other things causing you to feel this pressured. Something's wrong *inside you* if you overreact to mild stimulation. Let's sit down and pray."

I was skeptical but sat down on the sofa anyway and closed my eyes. Dennis said, "What's the first person or situation you see?" I saw myself as a child on the first day at a new school. In my gut, I could feel panicky apprehension about finding new friends, what the classes would be like, and if I'd like my teachers. When I told Dennis, he said, "From Jesus in you, receive forgiveness for carrying all that on your shoulders. It completely takes God out the picture." I received forgiveness and the panic left. I felt peace instead of anxiety. Next Dennis said, "Release the whole work situation into God's hands." From my gut, I relaxed and let it go. It felt like a river of release flowing out of my heart straight to God.

Dennis said, "How do you feel now?"

I told him, "I feel peaceful, like God and I can handle it together!"

Dennis asked, "Where did all the stress go?"

I replied, "I don't feel it anymore. It's gone! It must have been that old baggage making today seem too heavy for me to bear!"

I was amazed at the revelation that we can create our own stress because of unresolved issues from the past. Then, when everyday life happens, and it always does, we add current pressures on top of the old. Was I about to discover secrets that could set me free from the bane of modern existence—stress? I had just learned lesson number one.

> *We* can create our own stress because of unresolved issues from the past!

Stress has become an epidemic in modern society. The church is no different from the world in this respect. Almost no one is unscathed. Too many pastors and ministry leaders find themselves stressed to the point of exhaustion and often drop out of ministry altogether.

Stress is a three-way relationship between our demands on people (including ourselves) and circumstances, our feelings about those demands, and our ability to cope with them. A simple formula for understanding stress is: our excessive demands + our overwhelmed feelings + our inadequate ability = STRESS.

Notice that God is left out of this equation. Stress occurs when demands seem too great, we have too little control, and too little help appears to be available. In other words, the root of stress is our attempt to *control* life. However, when we're stressed, we're emotionally controlled by people or circumstances.

> *Stress* comes from our attempt to control life.

### Let It Go

When we take on burdens we were never meant to carry, we create our own stress (see Matt. 11:28). We often tell people they need to "let it go!" While that may be good advice, few people know *how* to do that.

Many years ago, when our daughter was a teenager, I (Jen) was very worried about her. You see, from the moment I was saved I was thrilled to know God had a plan for my life. Imagine my dismay with Allison announced that she didn't think she wanted God's will for her life. "What if it's His will for me be a missionary in some remote, primative village and live in a mud hut! I don't want to do that."

Dennis finally told me to let it go! I did know how to release something into the hands of God. So I sat down and prayed. However, the very next day, I found myself worrying about it again and told Dennis. He said, "I know you did it right yesterday, so tell me what you're thinking."

"I'm thinking, 'I'll give her to God but she can't miss God's will. I'll give her to God but she can't get in trouble with boys. I'll give her to God but she has to finish school.'"

Dennis replied, "I know what you're doing wrong. You're trying to release but you have strings attached. That's *conditional* release. Partial trust is not trust at all. You either give it to God or you don't. Let's try it again...the right way."

This time I gave her to God no matter what. I realized that even if she made mistakes, God was big enough to fix them. And this finally gave me lasting peace. Imagine my amazement when I watched God move like a whirlwind over the next few months and He put the pieces of her life together! Suddenly she wanted to do everything I had wanted her to do for years. And she announced that she *did* want God's will after all! I had learned lesson number two about freedom from stress. Worry is a form of control, and I had to let it go so God could work.

---

### PRACTICE
### HOW TO RELEASE

To release something to God, it is important to first understand that we must let it go in the heart. Second, when we release we are not being irresponsible and ceasing to care. Rather, we are taking our hands off (which is control), and placing the circumstance in the loving hands of God

- *Pray*. In an attitude of prayer, picture the person or situation.
- *Feel*. Feel the feeling in your gut.
- *Release*. Let release flow out (like forgiveness) toward God until you feel peace.

NOTE: Release can be compared to "dropping something on a conveyor belt" that takes it straight to God. Release is one of the rivers that flow from our belly (see John 7:38).

---

### *The Immune System*

Our body has two main survival mechanisms—one for *growth,* the immune system, and the other for *protection*, the stress response. Unfortunately, they can't operate simultaneously. When we are in growth mode, our body can grow and thrive. For our body to be healthy, the cells need to be well nourished and produce life-sustaining energy.

Growth is vitally important for your survival....
Every day billions of cells in your body wear out

and need to be replaced.... The entire lining of your gut is replaced every seventy-two hours. In order to maintain this continuous turnover of cells, your body needs to expend a significant amount of energy daily.[1]

The *immune system* protects the body against internal threats, such as bacteria and viruses. When our immune system is functioning properly, our body is in growth mode and our body is balanced and healthy. The immune system is connected to almost every other system of the body, and when the immune system isn't functioning optimally the rest of our body suffers. If we are stressed, our vitamins are flushed right out of our body. When we are at peace, the endothelial cells that line our blood vessels allow nutrients to pass from the capillaries to our cells.

> *When we are at peace, our blood vessels carry nutrients to our cells.*

### The HPA Axis

We switch to protective mode when our HPA (hypothalamus-pituitary-adrenal) axis is activated. The HPA axis is our "fight or flight" system to protect us against *external threats*. When we need extra speed or strength, bursts of energy from the HPA can be a good thing. It becomes a problem, however, if we live in protection mode all the time. When the HPA axis is activated by a threat, either real or imagined, stress hormones are released that guard against the threat but simultaneously inhibit our growth, health, and cognition.

Stress hormones override our biological tendency toward health. They limit the absorption of nutrients from the capillaries, constrict the blood vessels of the digestive tract, and interfere with blood flow in the brain, reducing awareness and decreasing general cognitive acuity. When we are stressed, we become less intelligent.

> *When* we are stressed, we
> become less intelligent.

Stress can be classified into two general categories—acute and chronic stress. *Acute stress* occurs in response to an immediate threat (the "fight or flight" response). The threat can be any short-term or emergency situation that, *even subconsciously or falsely*, is perceived as a danger. Acute stress in times of emergency is a good thing. However, *chronic stress* is "stress as a lifestyle," and our bodies are not designed to hold up under continuous pressure.

Research shows that chronic stress suppresses the action of the immune system, making us more vulnerable to disease. Our immune system can even turn against our own body in the form of autoimmune diseases or allergies.[2] Allergies are caused by judgments we have made against ourselves.

> *Chronic* stress is "stress as a lifestyle."

The negative effects of stress can be summed up in the following chart:

| Cognitive: | Emotional: |
|---|---|
| • Forgetfulness | • Touchy and overly sensitive |
| • Confusion | • Apathy or lethargy |
| • Indecision | • Restlessness and anxiety |
| • Inability to concentrate | • Inappropriate displays of laughter or crying |
| • Decreased intelligence | • Loss of confidence |
| • Uncharacteristic pessimism | • Depression |
| • Recurrent or runaway thoughts | • Anger and resentment |
| • Escapism | • Irritability |
| • Loss of objectivity | • Sense of being overwhelmed |
| • Impaired judgment | |
| **Behavioral:** | **Physical:** |
| • Changes in sleep patterns (increase or decrease) | • Digestive problems |
| • Eating more or less | • Grinding or gritting teeth |
| • Changes in sleep habits | • Headaches |
| • Lack of interest in normal socialization | • Insomnia |
| • Neglecting duties and responsibilities | • Fatigue |
| • Increase in alcohol or drug use | • Chest pain, irregular heartbeat |
| • Nervous habits (e.g., twisting hair, picking at cuticles) | • High blood pressure |
| • Explosions of anger | • Weight gain or loss |
| • Overreacting to people and life events | • Asthma or shortness of breath |
| | • Dermatitis and other skin problems |
| | • Decreased libido |

Many significant health issues are linked to chronic stress.[3] Indeed, stress is connected to virtually all leading causes of death, including cancer, heart disease, lung diseases, accidents, cirrhosis, and even suicide. Between 75–90 percent of all visits to primary care physicians are due to stress-related disorders.[4]

> *B*etween 75–90 percent of all visits to primary care physicians are due to stress.

Suppressing negative emotions instead of removing them through forgiveness is a prime factor in stress that leads to disease. Consider the words of Gabor Maté, MD, a Vancouver physician and the author of *When the Body Says No: The Cost of Hidden Stress.*[5] Here is an excerpt from an article Dr. Maté wrote:

> "I never get angry," says a character in one of Woody Allen's movies, "I grow a tumor instead." In over two decades of family medicine, including seven years of palliative care work, I have been struck by how consistently the lives of people with chronic illness are characterized by emotional shutdown: the paralysis of "negative" emotions—in particular, anger.
>
> This pattern holds true in a wide range of diseases from cancer, rheumatoid arthritis and multiple sclerosis to inflammatory bowel disorder, chronic fatigue syndrome, and amyotrophic lateral sclerosis (ALS).

The suppression of anger contributes to the onset of cancer and other diseases because the mind and body cannot be separated. The brain's emotional centres are directly and powerfully linked with the body's immune [system].[6]

### Adrenaline Addiction

I (Jen) am a hard worker. I loved being in school and getting A's. It gave me a great deal of satisfaction and I liked to get not only an A but the highest grade in my class. In the kingdom of God, however, our reward comes from much resting, not much striving. This was a lesson I would have to learn.

When Dennis and I began doing traveling ministry, I enjoyed all the projects and preparation. But I needed to learn that adrenaline was not anointing. Dennis called to me one day as I was rushing around and said, "I feel that we are supposed to be praying right now." I dutifully sat down, but found myself unable to feel the presence of God. I told Dennis, and he replied that *I* was the problem. "You need to receive forgiveness for that willpower energy. It attracts religious spirits!" I was horrified and received forgiveness immediately. As soon as I did, I felt the presence of God again.

Living in stress can become addictive. High levels of stress hormones generally make us feel uncomfortable and anxious. However, an individual may get used to living in a state of high alert and even enjoy the adrenaline "rush" produced. Eventually, the adrenaline addict may feel they need the energy and "mood boost" to function in everyday life.

Pressure, tension, frustration, anxiety, and a feeling of drivenness are *alarm signals* telling us something is not right and willpower has kicked in. However, some people rely on a dopamine[7] rush of excitement to relieve the feeling of pressure. While that may temporarily relieve the unpleasant sensation, it can lead to an addictive loop of "workaholism," competition, adventure (such as sky diving), religious striving, pornography, and so forth. After the initial high, feelings of frustration and anxiety quickly return, however. If the cycle isn't broken, it can continue until the individual burns out or becomes ill.

This pattern is not limited to secular society. An adrenaline rush can become a counterfeit of the anointing in ministry. When someone ministers under an anointing, they feel refreshed afterward. *Adrenaline energy* may feel similar to anointing, but often leads to a "crash" and exhaustion. Many people are reluctant to change because they enjoy getting high on willpower. However, stress hormones function like termites, eating away at the structure of the house. Even though the damage may occur silently, it is devastating nonetheless.

The antidote for stress due to over-excitement is yielding to God with thankfulness—maintaining an attitude of gratitude. When we are genuinely grateful to God, we tap into supernatural joy that energizes us by the Spirit. *"In everything give thanks; for this is the will of God in Christ Jesus for you"* (1 Thess. 5:18). And: *"The joy of the Lord is your strength"* (Neh. 8:10).

### Religious Spirits

Religious activities performed with willpower can cause stress. Adrenaline addiction in religion invites hitchhikers. Paul uses an unusual phrase translated "will worship" in the King James Version of the Bible. Will worship is the product of human willpower driven by religious spirits. Evil spirits enslave and condemn through religious rituals and man made tradition. *"If ye be dead with Christ from the rudiments of the world, why, as though living in the world, are ye subject to ordinances...after the commandments and doctrines of men? Which things have indeed a shew of wisdom in will worship"* (Col. 2:20-23 KJV).

The evil spirits driving idolatrous forms of worship are variously translated "elements" and "rudiments" in the King James Version of the Bible. The Greek word used here is *stoicheion*, referring to Gentile cults and Jewish theories and philosophies with the implication that animistic or demonic spirits ally with such religious rituals and traditions.[8] Religious spirits use rituals and commandments of man to bring us into bondage.

> *Even so we...were in bondage under the **elements** of the world* (Galatians 4:3).

> *Beware lest any man spoil you through philosophy and vain deceit, after the tradition of men, after the **rudiments** of the world, and not after Christ* (Colossians 2:8).

On the other hand, the Holy Spirit gently leads us into true worship and adoration of our God. It is not a "have to" but a "want to." Jesus tells us that true worship is both *"spirit and truth"* (John 4:24). What does that mean? The Greek for "truth" is *alētheia*, meaning "reality". This world is a mere illusion. We must turn to Jesus, the embodiment and perfection of truth, and true teaching of the gospel to be true worshipers. Next, we can only meet with God on His terms—spirit-to-Spirit.

The context of this statement in John 4 is a discussion about the subject of life-giving water; therefore, we can say that true spiritual worship is closely connected to God's personalized life-giving activity. When you offer your spirit to Him in praise and worship, His Spirit enlivens your spirit. New life flows into you from the Creator. Genuine worship occurs only when our human spirit, the immortal and invisible part of us, meets with God. It is the spirit of a man, through worship, which attains friendship and intimacy with God.[9]

## PRACTICE
### SELF-DELIVERANCE FROM A RELIGIOUS SPIRIT

If you are concerned about the possibility of religious spirits operating in your Christianity, close your eyes and pray. Picture your Christian life and service to God. If you feel peace and no particular area comes to mind, that's good. We are to let the peace of God rule in our life. If a particular aspect of religious activity or your Christianity in general stands out, feel the feeling in your gut. You might feel a particular negative emotion or just a sense of pressure.

A feeling of internal pressure or anxiety indicates we have been striving in willpower rather than living by the Spirit. When you picture any area (such as teaching Sunday school, witnessing, attending meetings, praying and reading your Bible "enough," doing charitable deeds, and so forth) and feel pressure inside, receive forgiveness until it changes to peace. We put most standards of religious performance on ourselves. If another person is involved, forgive the person. If you blame God, release forgiveness toward Him. Jesus says His burden is easy and His yoke is light (see Matt. 11:29-30).

If you still feel external pressure after you have peace in your heart, yield to Christ the deliverer in you, and welcome Him to rise up within you and push out any religious hitchhiker. Continue to yield to Him until you feel the pressure in the atmosphere lift.

## The Stress/Depression Connection

Depression is closely tied to stress and is often the result of too much unresolved stress. Depression also involves the *carnal options* for the will: 1) stressed? *"Fight or flight!"* or 2) depressed? *"Be a doormat!"* All the symptoms that are present for stress are present for depression—with a few additional symptoms.[10] Depression includes the following components: learned helplessness (giving up), loss of hope, anger turned inward (the feeling of being a "doormat"), and negative thinking patterns.

There is a *biological connection* between stress and depression. When pregnant mothers are stressed or depressed, their fetuses are more vulnerable to depression and anxiety when they grow older. In addition, they are at risk of developing learning and behavioral problems. Chronic *life stress* can also lead to depression, even in young children. When this link is formed, a child may be susceptible to depression throughout life. It is possible for a stress-depression link to lie dormant for long periods of time only to surface later due to prolonged stress or a traumatic event.[11]

*O*ver time, stress hormones damage the brain.

Dr. Vijai Sharma says, "New insights into the biological connection of depression trace it back to chronic and intolerable levels of emotional stress."[12] Over time, adrenal steroids (stress hormones) can harm brain structures. The parts of the brain responsible for emotions and memory are damaged because adrenal steroids inhibit the growth of nerve fibers in these areas. Chronic stress may cause the amygdala, the alarm system of the brain, to become enlarged.[13]

### Stress and the Will

In response to a stressful event, we generally believe we have three options. As mentioned previously, the three carnal responses are to fight back, run away, or to become a doormat—to simply give up. However, believers have a *fourth option*—to yield our will to God's will. We find an example of this in Luke 4:16-30. Jesus announced Himself as the Messiah in the synagogue and enraged those in attendance. The people present were "filled with wrath" and had every intention of throwing Jesus over a cliff. Jesus didn't fight them, run from them, or let them push Him off the cliff. He simply walked right through the crowd.

He was one and they were many. Why didn't they grab Him and stop Him? Because Jesus was under His Father's control, they were unable to touch Him. It was not the will of the Father for them to do so. *"Then passing through the midst of them, He went His way"* (Luke 4:30). When we are yielded to God, we are under His control.

> *W*hen we are yielded to God,
> we are under His control.

No one can control us if we are *yielded* to the will of God. When we are yielded to Him, we are at peace and have an inner assurance that He is in charge. As children of God, we should continually be yielded to Him.

### *Trusting or Trying?*

When I (Dennis) was a young believer, I learned how to release difficulties in my life into the hands of God and stay in peace. One time, my car transmission went out. Ordinarily, repairing or replacing a transmission is very expensive, and I only had $12.75 left in my checking account. Rather than become anxious, I released the situation to the Lord and felt peace. I said in my heart, "God, how are You going to take care of this?" When I took the car into the shop, the repairman said, "We have some transmission fluid that should solve the problem. It's twelve dollars." Because I relied upon God, He came through.

Biblical hope is synonymous with having an open heart. Hope functions like an anchor that keeps us connected to the presence of God (see Heb. 6:19). The state of "hope" is a product of staying open in our heart—being yielded to God. We can either *trust* or *try*—Spirit control or willpower control. It is impossible to trust God and be stressed at the same time. This is why the writer of Hebrews reminds us: *"Let us therefore be diligent to enter that rest"* (Heb. 4:11). Stress communicates *threat* and *fear*. Hope, on the other hand, communicates *trust* and *rest*; openness to God's control and resting in His ability is the opposite of *stress*.

*I*t is impossible to trust God and be stressed at the same time!

Jesus beckons us:

*Come to Me, all who are weary and heavy-laden, and I will give you rest. Take My yoke upon you and learn from Me, for I am gentle and humble in heart, and you will find rest for your souls. For My yoke is easy and My burden is light* (Matthew 11:28-30 NASB).

Abundant life is found in *trusting* and yielding to God. There is no trust in *trying* to control life through exerting our own will. The good news is that we can "let things go" and *release* them into the hands of God. When God is in control, we can relax. The antidote to stress is *trusting* God and *releasing* people (including yourself) and circumstances into His hands.

> *A*bundant life is found in *trusting* and yielding to God.

## PRACTICE

### FIVE KEYS FOR OVERCOMING STRESS

Stress should not be the normal way of life for Christians. We have a God who wants to set us free from stress-filled living. Learn to live in the peace of God instead of stress.

1. **Prayer.** 1) Set aside a daily prayer time to wait in the presence of the Lord. This will acclimate you to His presence and allow you to practice yielding your will to the Lord. 2) Ask the Lord to reveal past and present issues contributing to overall stress levels. 3) Spend a short time in prayer at the end of the day to deal with any unresolved situations so you don't carry today's trouble into tomorrow (see 1 John 1:9; Matt. 6:34).

   *Those who wait on the Lord shall renew their strength; they shall mount up with wings like eagles, they shall run and not be weary, they shall walk and not faint* (Isaiah 40:31).

2. **Past.** The undercurrent of repressed emotional baggage from the past can cause stress regardless of current life events. Set aside time on a regular basis for a while and concentrate on dealing with childhood and past issues. Many of our issues are hidden or forgotten, so the key is to allow God to reveal them to us in prayer. David asked God to search his heart and admitted that he had *secret faults* of which he himself was unaware.

   *Search me, O God, and know my heart; try me and know my anxious thoughts; and see if there be any hurtful way in me* (Psalm 139:23-24 NASB).

   *Who can understand his errors? Cleanse me from secret faults* (Psalm 19:12).

## PRACTICE

### FIVE KEYS FOR OVERCOMING STRESS (cont.)

*I acknowledged my sin to You, and my iniquity I did not hide. I said, I will confess my transgressions to the Lord [continually unfolding the past till all is told]—then You [instantly] forgave me* (Psalm 32:5 AMP).

3. **Present**. Learn to deal quickly with daily events of life. Anything that is not dealt with quickly is planted in the heart as a weed. Don't let it stay there and take root. If there is an overreaction to something, then take time to go to the Lord and ask Him to show you the root. If life pushes your buttons, you have the buttons in you. You can't change other people, but God can set *you* free.

   *Keep a sharp eye out for weeds of bitter discontent. A thistle or two gone to seed can ruin a whole garden in no time* (Hebrews 12:15 MSG).

   *Don't stay angry. Don't go to bed angry. Don't give the devil that kind of foothold in your life* (Ephesians 4:26 MSG).

4. **Peace**. Pay attention to any loss of peace. Pay attention whenever you feel anxiety and tension, and deal with it quickly. Your peace will instantly return when you 1) forgive and/or 2) release people and circumstances to God. Forgiveness "cleanses" the emotions and release gives control back to God.

   *Let the peace of God rule in your hearts* (Colossians 3:15).

5. **Path.** Practice walking in peace daily, step by step. Every time a stressful situation arises, release it back to the Lord. Every moment is a seed with potential for good when it is placed into the hands of God (see Rom. 8:28).

**PRACTICE**

**FIVE KEYS FOR OVERCOMING STRESS** (cont.)

*For shoes, put on the peace that comes from the Good News so that you will be fully prepared* (Ephesians 6:15 NLT).

*If we live in the Spirit, let us also walk in the Spirit* (Galatians 5:25).

*You will show me the path of life* (Psalm 16:11).

# ENDNOTES

1.  Lipton, *The Biology of Belief,* 145.

2.  B.S. McEwen, MD, "Protective and Damaging Effects of Stress Mediators," *The New England Journal of Medicine* 338, no. 3 (1998), 171–179.

3.  M. Jensen, "Psychobiological Factors Predicting the Course of Breast Cancer," *Journal of Personality* 55 (1987), 317–342; M. Larzelere and G. Jones, "Stress and Health," *Primary Care: Clinics in Office Practice* 35, no. 4 (2008), 839–856; Pennebaker, qtd. in Friedman, *Hostility, Coping, and Health,* 127–139; L. Temoshok, "Personality, Coping Style, Emotion, and Cancer: Toward an Integrative Model," *Cancer Surveys* 6 (1987), 545–567.

4.  D. Colbert, *Stress Less,* (Lake Mary, FL: Siloam Charisma Media/Charisma House Book Group, 2006), 5.

5.  G. Maté, *When the Body Says No: The Cost of Hidden Stress,* (Canada: Knopf, 2003).

6.  G. Maté, "Suppressing Our Emotions Harms Physical and Mental Health," (April 2004), Retrieved January 13, 2010 from *Alive,* http://www.alive.com/1787a5a2. php?subject_bread_cramb=78.

7.   Dopamine is a neuropeptide, or molecule of emotion, that helps control the brain's reward and pleasure centers. All addictions can be traced to dopamine-induced expectations, and it is responsible for the feeling of euphoria addicts seek.

8.   "Elements" [*stoicheion* in Greek] translates a Greek word, which originally referred to the triangle on a sundial for determining time by a shadow line. From there it came to be applied to going in order, advancing in steps or rows, elementary beginnings, and learning the letters of the alphabet. In NT usage, the word refers to the elementary principles of the OT (Heb. 5:12), the rudiments of both Jewish and Gentile religion (here and Col. 2:8, 20), and the material elements of the universe (2 Pet. 3:10,12).

Paul's use of the same word in verse 9. ("the weak and beggarly elements"), along with its usage in Col. 2, lends further insight into "elements." He teaches that spirits of the animistic or demonic dimension (verse 8) find easy allegiance with the rituals and philosophies of human religion and tradition. Hence, the elements of the world are actually evil spirits that use the rituals of the Law (verse 10) to enslave and condemn. [Footnote for Gal. 4:3: *Spirit-Filled Life Bible,* (Nashville: TN: Thomas Nelson Publishers, 1991), 1777.]

9.   S. Warren, *Unlocking the Heavens: Release the Supernatural Power of Your Worship,* (Shippensburg, PA: Destiny Image Publishers, Inc., 2014), 63-64.

10.  Symptoms of depression are identical to those of stress with some additional symptoms such as crying, sadness, hopelessness, and loss of pleasure in life.

11.  V.P. Sharma, "Stress-Depression Link Coming to Light," *Mind Publications* (December 2003), Retrieved April 3, 2007 from http://www.mindpub.com/art503.htm.

12.  Ibid.

13.  Ibid.

*Chapter 12*

# BIBLICAL HEALING

*Jesus, as Love Incarnate, walks among a suffering
humanity. In the midst of the suffering He
encounters, Love can do no less than reach out
to alleviate that suffering, to embrace, comfort,
and console. The presence of Love in the midst of
the world will always be a healing presence.*
—RICHARD MCALEAR[1]

Physical healing is a demonstration of the *power* of God most
certainly. However, it is also a sign of *who* Jesus is. As the Son of
God, He is holy and all-powerful, worthy of our reverence and
adoration. However, Jesus is a Savior who loves us immensely
and has great concern for us. The Gospels record numerous
occasions in which the heart of Jesus was moved with *compassion* when He observed the suffering multitudes.

The original word [*compassion*] is a very remarkable one. It is not found in classic Greek. It is not found in the Septuagint. The fact is, it was a word coined by the evangelists themselves. They did not find one in the whole Greek language that suited their purpose, and therefore they had to make one. It is expressive of the deepest emotion; a striving of the bowels—a yearning of the innermost nature with pity.[2]

Jesus was moved with a *yearning* to heal and comfort. His whole nature was greatly agitated and groaned on our behalf. "He gave up all the comforts of life—He gave His life itself; He gave His very self to prove that He was moved with compassion. Most of all do we see how He was moved with compassion in His terrible death."[3] When God heals us, it is a sign of His unfathomably great love! When we believe God's promises for healing, we honor Him as our God who *is* love.

---

*W*hen God heals us, it is a sign of
His unfathomably great love!

---

We see physical healing throughout the Bible. In the Old Testament Miriam was healed of leprosy when Moses prayed for her (see Num. 12:13). Job was healed when he forgave his friends. Both his prosperity and health were restored (see Job 42:10-13). Naaman humbled himself and was healed by an obedient action (see 2 Kings 5:1-15). The Old Testament also records other instances of individual healing.[4]

### Promises of Healing

Within the Old Testament, we find many promises of healing.[5] The Psalms promise healing.[6] In particular, in Psalm 103:2-3, David encourages us: *"Bless the Lord, O my soul, and forget not all His benefits: who forgives all your iniquities, who heals all your diseases."* Psalm 91:9-10 tells us that intimate fellowship with the Lord provides health protection: *"Because you have made the Lord...your dwelling place, no evil shall befall you, nor shall any plague come near your dwelling."*

Isaiah 53:4-5 prophesies of the coming Messiah and the promise of physical healing through His atonement:

> *Surely He has borne our griefs and carried our sorrows; yet we esteemed Him stricken, smitten by God, and afflicted. But He was wounded for our transgressions, He was bruised for our iniquities; the chastisement for our peace was upon Him, and by His stripes we are healed.*

Also, referring to this same prophecy, the apostle Peter writes: *"Who Himself bore our sins in His own body on the tree, that we, having died to sins, might live for righteousness—by whose stripes you were healed"* (1 Pet. 2:24).

In the New Testament, the biblical grounds for healing refer back to this prophecy in the Book of Isaiah. Matthew records:

> *When evening had come, they brought to Him many who were demon-possessed. And He cast out the spirits with a word, and healed all who were sick, that it might be fulfilled which was spoken by Isaiah the*

*prophet, saying: "He Himself took our infirmities and bore our sicknesses"* (Matthew 8:16-17).

---

"*He* Himself took our infirmities
and bore our sicknesses."

---

### Compassion for Healing

Under the New Covenant, the Lord expresses His *willingness* to heal those who are stricken with disease. A leper came to Jesus seeking healing, but he wasn't quite sure that Jesus was favorably inclined to heal him. We get a glimpse not only of Jesus's *power* to heal but of His *compassion* for healing as well:

> *Now a leper came to Him, imploring Him, kneeling down to Him and saying to Him, "If You are willing, You can make me clean." Then Jesus, moved with compassion, stretched out His hand and touched him, and said to him, "I am willing; be cleansed"* (Mark 1:40-42).

God is concerned about the restoration of every part of us. This is one of the reasons the apostle Paul says God wants to make our spirit, soul, *and* body completely whole: *"Now may the God of peace Himself sanctify you completely; and may your whole spirit, soul, and body be preserved blameless at the coming of our Lord Jesus Christ"* (1 Thess. 5:23); and why John prays for much the same thing: *"Beloved, I pray that you may prosper in all things and be in health, just as your soul prospers"* (3 John 1:2).

*G*od wants to make *every* part of us whole.

The Gospels record 41 distinct instances of healing. However, there is no way to know how many total individuals were included in the "multitudes" delivered and healed. What we do know for certain is that healing was an important part of Jesus's ministry. On more than one occasion, the gospel writers sum up Jesus's ministry by showing that He healed those who came to Him:

> *And Jesus went about all Galilee, teaching in their synagogues, preaching the gospel of the kingdom, and healing all kinds of sickness and all kinds of disease among the people* (Matthew 4:23).

> *But when the multitudes knew it, they followed Him; and He received them and spoke to them about the kingdom of God, and healed those who had need of healing* (Luke 9:11).

> *And the whole multitude sought to touch Him, for power went out from Him and healed them all* (Luke 6:19).

The apostle John tells us: *"There are also many other things that Jesus did, which if they were written one by one, I suppose that even the world itself could not contain the books that would be written"* (John 21:25).

---

### *"Power* went out from Him
### and healed them all."

---

### *Different Ways of Healing*

Physical healing may take place in many different ways. The Scriptures record various means by which individuals were healed, so we cannot make a "rule" or religious absolute. The following are examples of some of the ways Jesus healed:

> *The centurion answered and said, "Lord, I am not worthy that You should come under my roof. But only* **speak a word**, *and my servant will be healed.... Then Jesus said to the centurion,* **"Go your way; and as you have believed, so let it be done for you."** *And his servant was healed that same hour* (Matthew 8:8,13).

> *Now when Jesus had come into Peter's house, He saw his wife's mother lying sick with a fever. So He* **touched her hand**, *and the fever left her. And she arose and served them* (Matthew 8:14-15).

> *And suddenly, a woman who had a flow of blood for twelve years came from behind and touched the hem of His garment. For she said to herself,* **"If only I may touch His garment, I shall be made well."** *But Jesus turned around, and when He saw her He said, "Be of good cheer, daughter;* **your faith has made you well."** *And the woman was made well from that hour* (Matthew 9:20-22).

*And **Jesus rebuked the demon**, and it came out of him; **and the child was cured** from that very hour* (Matthew 17:18).

*He said to the man, **"Stretch out your hand."** And he stretched it out, and his hand was restored as whole as the other* (Mark 3:5).

*Then they brought to Him one who was deaf and had an impediment in his speech, and they begged Him to put His hand on him. And **He took him aside from the multitude, and put His fingers in his ears, and He spat and touched his tongue*** (Mark 7:32-33).

*When He had said these things, He spat on the ground and made clay with the saliva; and **He anointed the eyes of the blind man with the clay. And He said to him, "Go, wash in the pool of Siloam"*** (which is translated, Sent). *So he went and washed, and came back seeing* (John 9:6-7).

### Believers' Authority to Heal

Jesus not only healed people Himself, He imparted the power to heal to His disciples. During His time on earth, *"He called His twelve disciples together and gave them power and authority over all demons, and to cure diseases. He sent them to preach the kingdom of God and to heal the sick"* (Luke 9:1-2).

> *J*esus gave believers power and authority to heal the sick.

*And they cast out many demons, and **anointed with oil many who were sick**, and healed them* (Mark 6:13).

After the Resurrection, Jesus charged His followers to *continue* with the ministry of healing: *"And these signs will follow those who believe: In My name they will cast out demons...they will lay hands on the sick, and they will recover"* (Mark 16:17-18).

The disciples of Jesus can heal. Throughout the Book of Acts and the Epistles, we find many accounts of believers ministering healing.[7]

James 5:14 explains how to access divine healing: *"Is anyone among you sick? Let him call for the elders of the church, and let them pray over him, anointing him with oil in the name of the Lord."* James further instructs believers: *"Confess your trespasses to one another, and pray for one another, that you may be healed. The effective, fervent prayer of a righteous man avails much"* (James 5:16).

Scripture clearly states that spiritual gifts also may be imparted to believers for healing: *"To another faith by the same Spirit, to another gifts of healings by the same Spirit"* (1 Cor. 12:9). Certain healings recorded in the Book of Acts occur in conjunction with *faith actions*. *"Peter said, 'Silver and gold I do not have, but what I do have I give you: In the name of Jesus Christ of Nazareth, rise up and walk'"* (Acts 3:6).

### Unusual Healing Miracles

Some *unusual* healing miracles were accomplished through believers in the Book of Acts as well. Believers laid those who were ill on beds and couches in the streets so they would be healed as Peter's shadow fell on them (see Acts 5:15) and cloths that had touched Paul's skin were placed on those who were sick and they were healed and delivered (see Acts 19:11-12).

The Bible records two clear instances of individuals drawing *directly* on the healing power of Jesus. The woman with the issue of blood *drew on the healing power of Jesus* by faith in order to be healed.

*And a woman who had suffered from a flow of blood for twelve years and had spent all her living upon physicians, and could not be healed by anyone, came up behind Him and touched the fringe of His garment, and immediately her flow of blood ceased. And Jesus said, Who is it who touched Me? When all were denying it, Peter and those who were with him said, Master, the multitudes surround You and press You on every side! But Jesus said, Someone did touch Me; for I perceived that [**healing**] **power** has gone forth from Me* (Luke 8:43-46 AMP).

When the apostle Paul was aboard a Roman ship, a storm caused them to shipwreck on the island of Malta (see Acts 28). While Paul gathered wood and placed it on the fire, a poisonous snake bit him (see Acts 28:2–5). The natives expected Paul to die, but, to their amazement, he just shook the viper off and was unharmed.[8] He didn't kneel down and say prayers to God in heaven, and the elders didn't come pray for him or anoint him with oil.

However, Paul, surely received healing power from the Divine Healer. We believe it is possible that Paul yielded to the Healer in his own heart. We too can receive anointing for healing, whether from God in heaven, impartation from the laying on of hands, or yielding to the Healer in our own heart. Regardless of how we approach the Lord, the Scriptures tell us that, when we turn to God in faith, we can trust Him.

> *If a son asks for bread from any father among you, will he give him a stone? Or if he asks for a fish, will he give him a serpent instead of a fish? Or if he asks for an egg, will he offer him a scorpion? If you then, being evil, know how to give good gifts to your children, how much more will your heavenly Father give the Holy Spirit to those who ask Him!* (Luke 11:11-13).

Of course, this doesn't mean we should be "lone rangers" who never seek prayer from others. However, we should not be so dependent on the gifts of others that we don't have confidence to rely upon Christ in us. The Bible assures us: *"And my God shall supply all your need according to His riches in glory by Christ Jesus"* (Phil. 4:19).

Both Paul and the woman with the issue of blood *drew* healing power from Jesus. We can also draw healing power from Christ the Divine Healer in our heart when we have need of healing.

*We* **can yield to the Divine Healer in our heart for healing.**

# ENDNOTES

1. R. McAlear, *The Power of Healing Prayer: Overcoming Emotional and Psychological Blocks*, (South Bend, IN: Our Sunday Publisher, 2012), 12.

2. C. Spurgeon, "The Compassion of Jesus," *The Spurgeon Archive* No. 3438, (December 24, 1914). Retrieved March 25, 2015 from http://www.spurgeon.org/sermons/3438.htm.

3. Ibid.

4. At least 12 instances of individual healings are recorded in the Old Testament as well: Gen. 20:1-8; Num. 12:1-15; 1 Sam. 1:19-20; 1 Kings 13:4-6; 17:17-24; 2 Kings 4:18-37; 5:1-14; 13:21; 20:1-7; Job 42:10-17; Dan. 4:34,36. Three corporate healings are mentioned (see Num. 16:46-50; 21:4-9; 2 Sam. 24:10-25). In addition, God healed a women of barrenness (see Gen. 18:10,14; 21:1-3; Judg. 13:5-25; 1 Sam. 1:19-20).

5. See Exod. 23:25-26; Deut. 7:15; Hos. 6:1-2; Isa. 29:18; 33:24; 35:5-6; 53:5; 61:1-3; Ezek. 47:12; Mal. 4:2.

6. See Ps. 42:1-3; 116:3-6; 147:3.

7. See Acts 3:1-6; 5:12; 5:15; 6:8; 8:5-8; 9:17-18; 9:32-34; 9:36-42; 14:7-10; 14:19-28; 20:7-12; 28:7-8; Phil. 2:25-30; 4:15-19.

8. After the Resurrection, Jesus declared that signs and wonders would follow those who believe, including not being harmed by deadly serpents (see Mark 16:17-18).

*Chapter 13*

# PRINCIPLES OF HEALING

A miracle is an instant work of God. Healing, on the other hand, may be progressive. Regardless of the time element involved, we must keep our heart open. For example, when the Lord healed me of eczema after I (Jen) forgave classmates from elementary school, my skin became clearer every day for several weeks until the eczema was gone. When God brought healing to a damaged nerve in my face, it was an instantaneous miracle.

When Jesus touched Peter's mother-in-law, a healing *miracle* occurred:

> *Now when Jesus had come into Peter's house, He saw his wife's mother lying sick with a fever. So He touched her hand, and the fever left her. And she arose and served them* (Matthew 8:14-15).

In this account, Jesus prayed *twice* before healing was complete.

*Then [Jesus] came to Bethsaida; and they brought a blind man to Him, and begged Him to touch him. So He took the blind man by the hand and led him out of the town. And when He had spit on his eyes and put His hands on him, He asked him if he saw anything. And he looked up and said, "I see men like trees, walking." Then He put His hands on his eyes again and made him look up. And he was restored and saw everyone clearly* (Mark 8:22-25).

Another progressive healing happened when Jesus prayed for ten lepers in the Gospel of Luke. He told them to go to the priests, and they were healed as they went.

*Now it happened as He went to Jerusalem that He passed through the midst of Samaria and Galilee. Then as He entered a certain village, there met Him ten men who were lepers, who stood afar off. And they lifted up their voices and said, "Jesus, Master, have mercy on us!" So when He saw them, He said to them, "Go, show yourselves to the priests." And so it was that as they went, they were cleansed* (Luke 17:11-14).

## SEVEN HELPS AND HINDRANCES TO HEALING

### 1. *Don't Give Up*

When believing God for healing, we shouldn't give up. Biblical hope may be defined as "keeping the heart open," which means that belief requires an open heart. When our heart is closed, we can receive nothing. We can only receive what we are open to. The writer of Proverbs reminds us, *"Hope deferred makes the heart sick, but when the desire comes, it is a tree of life"* (Prov. 13:12). And Jesus said, *"You must regularly ask and it will be given to you, you must continually seek and you will find, you must knock habitually and it will be opened to you"* (Matt. 7:7 ONMB)

> *"Shutting down" closes your connection to God.*

## 2. Release Any Judgments against God

We *must* avoid becoming angry with God if He doesn't do what we want Him to do, when we want Him to do it. If we are angry with the Lord, we have cut off the connection with our source of help. Anger creates a barrier that prevents God from working on our behalf. What must we do? Forgive God. When we forgive God, it is important to remember that He didn't do anything wrong. We simply release any judgments we have made against Him.

## 3. Ask God

Every believer should be led by the Lord when healing is needed. There are no ironclad rules to adhere to. We must be like David who continually "inquired of the Lord." God never gave David the same strategy twice. Job was healed when he prayed for his friends: *"And the Lord turned the captivity of Job and restored his fortunes, when he prayed for his friends"* (Job 42:10 AMP). Naaman, who was the commander of the army of the king of Syria, was healed of leprosy when he humbled himself and dipped in the Jordan River seven times (see 2 Kings 5:1-14).

*Inquire of the Lord.*

### 4. Yield to the Divine Healer Within

In the 1990s, it became a popular practice for believers to participate in what is called "soaking" in the presence of God. Christians meeting together as a group or alone in their homes felt prompted to play worship music and spend time yielding to the presence of the Lord. Soaking is simply a new term for "waiting" before God.[1] As noted previously, soaking is an effective way to pursue healing.

When we pray for others, the person suffering from a physical condition should be encouraged to yield to the Divine Healer in them, while others let rivers of healing flow out from them to the afflicted person (see John 7:38). That is truly a spiritual "prayer of agreement" rather than mental assent (see Matt. 18:19-20).

### 5. Persevere

Don't impose a time limit on God. Allow God to determine the timing. The same God who formed us in our mother's womb understands how we are made, where the knots are, and how to untangle them (see Ps. 139:13-16). In the same way that mental strongholds may be described as a "house of thoughts," *several* emotional issues may be a barrier to healing. God may deal with one issue at one time, and another issue at another time, until finally He removes the last tangle—and suddenly healing manifests.

*D*on't put a time limit on God!

### 6. Walk in Self-Deliverance

Healing for some diseases requires deliverance from spiritual hitchhikers, such as a spirit of infirmity or a spirit of death. A spiritual hitchhiker requires emotional legal ground, or permission, to remain. When we deal with a toxic emotion through forgiveness, we close the door and take back the ground given over to the enemy.

If you suspect a hitchhiker is involved, close your eyes and pray. Ask God, "Where did this come in?" Pray through the steps of forgiveness (first, feel, forgive) until you get peace where there was a negative emotion, and the hitchhiker cannot stay. If you feel any lingering bad presence, yield to Christ the deliverer in you and allow Him to fill you from head to toe, "pushing out" any torment.

If you feel peace inside your heart, but still feel an unpleasant atmosphere outside of you, resist opening the door to let it back in. Submit to God, resist the devil, and he must flee (see James 4:7). Guard your thought and emotion doors by refusing to give in to any lingering intrusive thoughts or outside pressure.

*G*uard your thought and emotion doors.

## 7. Fellowship with God

Jesus says that our relationship with Him can be likened to the way a branch connects to a vine. We stay connected with Jesus in our heart by learning to abide in Him.

> *I am the Vine; you are the branches. Whoever lives [abides] in Me and I in him bears much (abundant) fruit. However, apart from Me [cut off from vital union with Me] you can do nothing* (John 15:5 AMP).

When a branch is connected to the vine, it taps into its life source. If a branch is disconnected from the vine, it begins to wither because it no longer has life flowing through it. The *stronger* the connection, the healthier the branch. The more life flowing through the branch, the more fruit it can bear.

When we live in the Spirit, our whole being continually touches the presence of God. We *abide*, or dwell, in Christ. When our soul—mind, will, and emotions—is ruled by Christ, everything in our life will begin to prosper, including our physical health: *"Beloved, I pray that you may prosper in all things and be in health, just as your soul prospers"* (3 John 1:2).

*We* **must stay connected to God to thrive.**

The Bible tells us that the blood that flowed from the stripes on Jesus's back paid the price for physical healing: *"By His stripes we are healed"* (Isa. 53:5). A stripe is the wound from a whip that tears the skin so blood flows. The Hebrew word for "stripe" is *havura*. "At least one translation used by Orthodox Jews translates this as fellowship; we are healed by fellowship with Him. That is true because we serve a God of relationship."[2]

Therefore, we don't just receive *healing anointing* as a "something," we are healed through relationship with *Someone*. When we abide in Christ, we live in communion with the One who heals. Sid Roth explains, "The best way to get a healing is through having intimacy and relationship—fellowship with God. It's because of His blood that we are healed. But it is because of our fellowship that we have a clear passageway for the healing to manifest in our body."[3]

---

*H*ealing comes through
relationship with the Healer!

---

## ENDNOTES

1. When I (Dennis) was a new believer, the Holy Spirit taught me to "wait with specificity" in the presence of the Lord. For example, when God was healing me of rejection, I soaked in His acceptance and "undivided attention." That purged rejection out of me and filled me with an anointing of acceptance. When I needed physical healing, I welcomed the Divine Healer into that area of my body.

2. Morford, *The One New Man Bible,* 1741. William Morford sheds additional light on this passage of Scripture when he writes:

   Isaiah 53:5 has an unusual twist because the word translated wounds or stripes is listed in modern Hebrew dictionaries with a different meaning. The word is Havurah. The confusion comes because another root, H-v-r, relates to fellowship, so at least one modern English translation used by Orthodox Jewish congregations in the U.S. translates this as fellowship, that we have been healed by fellowship with Him. That is true, because we serve the God of relationship.... Havurah literally means sore, but stripe(s) or wound(s) are appropriate translations. In Isaiah's time all his readers understood that as stripes or wounds, but now we see more depth in those words.... Remember that relationship with Him is what this is all about, a subliminal message in Isaiah 53:5.

3. S. Roth, television interview with William J. Morford, *It's Supernatural!*, March 14, 2014.

*Chapter 14*

# DIVINE HEALTH

What if there were something more than just praying and believing for *healing*? Is it possible to have Divine Health? Is it possible for an *entire nation* to enjoy perfect health? Yes! That is exactly what the Bible tells us! When God delivered the Israelites after 430 years of slavery in Egypt, not a single feeble, crippled, or sickly person was counted among them. Psalm 105 tells us that God *"brought them out with silver and gold, and there was none feeble among His tribes.... He brought out His people with joy, His chosen ones with gladness"* (Ps. 105:37,43).

> *"There was none feeble among His tribes."*

In Egypt their spirits had become embittered, but God led them forth with joy in their hearts. The Israelites had been impoverished slaves, but God enriched them with gifts of gold and silver. Their bodies had been abused and broken with hard labor, but God gifted them with health and healing. When the Israelites came out of Egypt no one was sick. No one was crippled. No one even needed assistance to walk. This included every man, woman, and child, from the oldest to the youngest. What other nation in history has had such a testimony?

Prior to the Exodus, God had visited Egypt with a series of nine plagues, none of which had harmed the Jewish people.[1] God now announced the tenth and final plague—the death of the firstborn son. He then provided salvation from the plague for His people through the blood of a sacrificial lamb and a Passover meal, which pointed to the coming Passover Lamb—the Lord Jesus Christ (see Exod. 12:3-28).

> The movement of the Israelites from slaves of Pharaoh to servants of the Lord involves divine redemption; it also involves the obedient response of God's people to His word. The Passover is both bloody and beautiful. God's judgment and salvation are clearly displayed in God's actions and in the symbolism of the Passover ritual. The atonement of Christ is both bloody and beautiful.... Through the Passover God consecrated the Israelites as His atoned for, purified, and sanctified people (Ex. 19:6). This event marked the beginning of Israel's new life as they headed for Mount Sinai and eventually the promised land.[2]

Recall what was included in the atonement of Jesus Christ. He offered Himself as sacrifice for our sins but also paid the price for our deliverance *"from this present evil age"* (Gal. 1:4). Sickness and disease are clearly the result of the Fall and part of the evil in the world. Isaiah tells us that Jesus was *"led as a lamb to the slaughter"* (Isa. 53:7), and due to His sacrifice on our behalf, *"by His stripes we are healed"* (Isa. 53:5).

> *For this purpose the Son of God was manifested, that He might destroy the works of the devil* (1 John 3:8).

## "*B*y His stripes we are healed."

It is a great blessing for the sick to be healed. However, the Bible also gives examples of those who enjoyed divine health that even defied the natural aging process. Sarah became pregnant and gave birth to a son when Abraham was 100 and she was 90 (see Gen. 21:2). Although Moses was 120 years old immediately before Joshua led the children of Israel into the Promised Land, the Scriptures tell us that *"his eyesight was clear, and he was as strong as ever"* (Deut. 34:7 NLT).

When Caleb was 40, God promised him the land of Hebron. At the time the Israelites finally entered the Promised Land, Caleb was age 85. Nevertheless, Caleb said to Joshua:

> *Now, as you can see, the Lord has kept me alive and well as He promised for all these forty-five years since Moses made this promise—even while Israel wandered in the wilderness. Today I am eighty-five years old. I*

*am as strong now as I was when Moses sent me on*
*that journey, and I can still travel and fight as well as*
*I could then. So give me the hill country that the Lord*
*promised me* (Joshua 14:10-12 NLT).

The Bible uses *types* to point to future fulfillment. The offering of Abel pointed to the sacrifice of Christ. Boaz in the Book of Ruth is a type of Christ, our Kinsman-Redeemer. Israel crossing the Jordan is a picture of the believer entering into a victorious Christian life. Enoch is a type of the Christian who will draw so close to God that he or she will be translated and not know death. The physical health of the Israelites points to an end time company of believers who will overcome sickness and disease because they know their Divine Healer intimately.

What would it mean for the body of Christ if we could *live in Divine Health*?

### *Divine Health*

In his book *The Eternal Church*, Dr. Bill Hamon prophesied that a time would come when God would release a wave of resurrection life that would bring not just more and greater gifts of healing, but it would release *Divine Health* for the body of Christ.[3] In fact, we believe that time has come. When believers have a revelation of Christ the Divine Healer within, they understand that we can go directly to Him. God has already given us access to His healing power in our own heart.

A supernatural flow of divine life will come into the...Church a few years prior to the time of translation. This will not initially be for the bodily immortalization of the saints. It will enable the

Church to demonstrate Jesus Christ, not only as Savior of man, but as Lord of all.... Super-abundant resurrection life shall be divinely imparted in order to demonstrate that the Head of the Church is living in His Corporate Body as a supernatural resurrected Christ.[4]

The Scriptures about life, death, and immortality will be fulfilled in a generation of those who appropriate promises relegated to the future and draw them into present-day fulfillment. Truths that have seemed like ethereal poetry will become living reality.[5]

*This will be written for the generation to come, that a people yet to be created may praise the Lord. For He looked down from the height of His sanctuary; from heaven the Lord viewed the earth, to hear the groaning of the prisoner, to release those appointed to death* (Psalm 102:18-20).

All hindrances to the believer's deliverance clear up to total glorification...[are on] the human side. One man, Enoch, proved, verified, and confirmed this principle by appropriating faith for glorification (Gen. 5:24; Heb. 11:5). Enoch's experience proves that there is a legal basis for full deliverance in this life from every result of the Fall for every child of God.[6]

*We want to be...further clothed, that mortality may be swallowed up by life* (2 Corinthians 5:4).

> *A*ll hindrances to the believer's
> deliverance are on the human side.

The Bible assures us that healing is the "children's bread" (see Mark 7:27). And: *"Give attention to my words; incline your ear to my sayings.... Keep them in the midst of your heart; for they are life to those who find them, and health to all their flesh"* (Prov. 4:20-22). Receive the promises of God today and appropriate your inheritance of Divine Health and healing!

## ENDNOTES

1. See Exod. 7:14; 8:1,16,20; 9:1,8,13; 10:1; 12:29.

2. M. Capps, "The Atonement and the Passover: Exodus 12," *Christianity Today*, Apr 29, 2014. Retrieved September 18, 2014 from http://www.christianitytoday.com/edstetzer/2014/april/atonement-and-passover-exodus-12-by-matt-capps.html.

3. W.S. Hamon, *The Eternal Church*, (Phoenix, AZ: Christian International Publishers, 1981), 336.

4. Ibid., 335-336.

5. Ps. 102:16-21; 1 Cor. 15:26,42,54; 2 Cor. 5:4; Rom. 8:21; 2 Tim. 1:10.

6. P. Billheimer, *Don't Waste Your Sorrows*, (Fort Washington, PA: Christian Literature Crusade, 1977), 103.

*Chapter 15*

# DIVINE LIGHT

According to research done by Dr. Fritz-Albert Popp, physicist and professor at Marburg University in Germany, all living organisms emit tiny particles of light called biophotons.[1] What does that mean for us? He quantified what scientists have long suspected, that life and light are connected. According to Dr. Popp, human beings are "created to be *beings of light*. We are still on the threshold of fully understanding the complex relationship between light and life, but we can now say emphatically, that the function of our entire metabolism is dependent on light."[2]

The modern science of photobiology is presently proving this. In terms of healing the implications are immense. We now know, for example, that quanta of light can initiate, or arrest, cascade-like reactions in the cells, and that genetic cellular damage can be virtually repaired, within hours, by faint beams of light.[3]

---

## *We* are created to be beings of light.

---

What does this mean for us spiritually? All beings have a lesser light. However, the Greater Light has revealed Himself to us. In the natural, human light is exceedingly dim, but the Bible tells us that we will someday *"shine forth as the sun in the kingdom"* of God (Matt. 13:43). We are made to be bearers of the *light of God*.

> *The path of the just is like the shining sun, that shines ever brighter unto the perfect day* (Proverbs 4:18).

### The Light of the World

As soon as we think of light, we automatically think of the sun. It is the center of our solar system and the light that gives life to our natural world. However, the Son who created the sun came to earth and announced Himself as the Light of the world: *"I am the Light of the world. He who follows Me shall not walk in darkness, but have the light of life"* (John 8:12).

Consider this description of the Light of the world in Hebrews 1:3 in the Amplified translation of the Bible:

> *He is the sole expression of the glory of God [the Light-being, the out-raying or radiance of the divine], and He is the perfect imprint and very image of [God's] nature, upholding and maintaining and guiding and*

*propelling the universe by His mighty word of power. When He had by offering Himself accomplished our cleansing of sins and riddance of guilt, He sat down at the right hand of the divine Majesty on high.*

> *T*he Son who created the sun
> came as the Light of the world.

Throughout the Scriptures heavenly beings are described in terms of light. An angel appeared to the shepherds in the field to announce the birth of Jesus and *"the glory"* shone around them (see Luke 2:8-9). God wraps Himself with light as a garment (see Ps. 104:2). The Book of Revelation tells us the face of Jesus is *"like the sun shining in its strength"* (Rev. 1:16).

While Jesus was on earth, He took on the appearance of a natural man. In only one instance in Jesus's earth walk did He allow His heavenly glory to be revealed. Jesus led Peter, James, and John to a high mountain *"and He was transfigured before them. His face shone like the sun, and His clothes became as white as the light"* (Matt. 17:2).

As the Light of the world, Jesus gave life to the world. Not only did He bring hope, comfort, freedom, and healing to humankind but *"abolished death and brought life and immortality to light through the gospel"* (2 Tim. 1:10). Jesus also came to be a Father to *sons*, not just to forgive our sins and take us to heaven someday. And what kind of sons would these be? Sons restored to the glory of God, of course. The *"Captain"* of our salvation came to bring *"many sons to glory"* (Heb. 2:10). God is the *"Father of lights"* (James 1:17). We are *"children of light"* (Eph. 5:8). Christ in us is *our* hope of regaining the lost glory (see Col. 1:27).

---

*C*hrist in us is *our* hope of glory.

---

### Children of Light

The glory of God is the core brilliance of His manifest presence. In the Garden of Eden, Adam and Eve were clothed in the glory. The glory filled the atmosphere of the Garden and covered them completely. They didn't wear physical clothing; they were enveloped in a spiritual garment (see Gen. 2:25). When they lost the glory, they realized they were naked and were ashamed (see Gen. 3:7).

Jesus not only came for forgiveness of sin and to bring us relief from emotional and physical torment, but to restore us to our original standing as sons and daughters of the Living God: *"All have sinned and fall short of the glory of God"* (Rom. 3:23). Forgiveness takes care of our sin problem but we are also promised the glory. Jesus came to bring sons and daughters back to the *fullness* of light—to the glory that was lost (see Heb. 2:10). We can once again be clothed in God's glory by putting on *"the armor of light...the Lord Jesus Christ"* (Rom. 13:12-14).

The Scriptures say that Father God has qualified us to *"share in the inheritance of His holy people in the kingdom of light"* (Col. 1:12 NIV). The Holy Spirit in us *"bears witness with our spirit that we are children of God, and if children, then heirs—heirs of God and joint heirs with Christ"* (Rom. 8:16-17). What does this inheritance consist of? We are heirs of everything lost by Adam and Eve due to sin, including the glory of God.

In John 17, Jesus prayed to Father God: *"The glory which You gave Me I have given them"* (John 17:22). Jesus says He has *already* given us access to His glory. Therefore, any failure to receive the glory is on our part!

*J*esus has *already* given us access to the glory.

Jesus came not only to reveal Himself as who He is, but to demonstrate to us what human beings could become in Christ. In other words, Jesus came to earth in human form, having emptied Himself. As Son of Man He lived entirely by the power of the Holy Spirit in Him, not by His own power as Deity. As such, He revealed to us our spiritual potential and inheritance as heirs of Christ. Jesus did not come to lower Himself to our level, but to lift us up to where He is by grace (see Eph. 2:6). Grace is so much more than "unmerited favor." It is the power of Christ Himself living His life through us.

> God's ultimate purpose for us is for our self-life to be completely taken up and transformed into Christ's life. When we came to Christ, we died with Him. We have died to our old way of life and now *"our life is hid with Christ in God." "I live; yet not I that liveth but Christ that liveth in me..." "that the life also of Jesus might be made manifest in our body...in our mortal flesh"* (Gal. 2:20; 2 Cor. 4:10-11; Col. 3:3).[4]

What is the intent of our Messiah, the *"Light-being, the out-raying or radiance of the Divine,"* for humankind (see Heb. 1:3 AMP)? To restore us to the glory forfeited by Adam and Eve and to bring us to *full* glorification.

> *We all, with unveiled face, beholding as in a mirror the glory of the Lord, are being transformed into the same image from glory to glory, just as by the Spirit of the Lord* (2 Corinthians 3:18).

### The Divine Light Within

Those who discover the power of the Divine Healer within herald the beginning of a new season for the church of Jesus Christ. Believers are created to be bearers of the light of the glory of God. In His Light we find life, healing, and health. *"To you who fear My name the Sun of Righteousness shall arise with healing in His wings"* (Mal. 4:2).

Arise in faith and enter into the promises of God for the redemption of the whole person—spirit, soul, and *body* (see 1 Thess. 5:23)!

> *Arise, shine; for your light has come! And the glory of the Lord is risen upon you* (Isaiah 60:1).

## ENDNOTES

1. All matter is created from atoms and molecules. The atom is the smallest unit of matter and a molecule is the smallest particle in a chemical element, composed of two or more atoms. Atoms have a nucleus made of protons and neutrons and one or more elections orbiting the nucleus. The nucleus forms the mass of the atom. If you picture the planets orbiting

around the sun, the nucleus would be the sun and the electrons would be the planets. The solid objects that we can see and touch are made of particles of energy. If you could see into the tiny world of the atom, you would see vast amounts of "empty" space between each component. In other words, matter has more space than solid. What appears to be solid matter is actually made of energy.

2.    A.F. Popp, K. Li, and Q. Gu, "Recent Advances in Biophoton Research and Its Application," *World Scientific* (1992), 1-18; F.A Popp, G. Quao, and L. Ke-Hsuen, "Biophoton Emission: Experimental Background and Theoretical Approaches," *Modern Physics Letters B*, 8 (1994), 21-22; F.A. Popp, et al., "Evidence of non-classical (squeezed) light in biological systems," *Modern Physics Letters A*, 239, nos. 1 and 2 (2002), 98–102; S. Cohen and F.A. Popp, "Biophoton Emission of the Human Body," *Journal of Photochemistry and Photobiology B: Biology* 40, no. 2 (1997), 187–189.

3.    "Prof. Fitz-Albert Popp," *Biophoton Light Arizona*. Retrieved March 5, 2014 from http://biontologyarizona.com/dr-fritz -albert-popp/.

4.    W.S. Hamon, *The Eternal Church,* (Point Washington, FL: Christian International, 1981), 36.

*Prayer Card/Troubleshooting Card*

*on next page.*

⟶

## RELEASING THE DIVINE HEALER WITHIN
# PRAYER CARD

### 1. Pray

Prayer is fellowship with a Person. Come into the presence of the Divine Healer to honor Him.

- *Pray.* Close your eyes and pray, placing your hand on your belly.
- *Focus.* Focus on Christ within.
- *Feel peace.* Yield and feel peace.

### 2. Receive

- *Pray.* Close your eyes and pray, placing your hand on your belly.
- *Yield.* Yield to the Divine Healer in your heart.
- *Receive.* Welcome healing into every cell of your body.

### 3. Soak

- *Time.* Set aside a period of time—at least thirty minutes—and wait quietly in the presence of the Divine Healer.
- *Yield.* Yield even more and go deeper in God. The more you open your spirit to God, the faster the healing can occur.

### 4. Remove Barriers

Negative emotions are barriers to healing. Forgiveness removes negative emotions. If you are angry at God, start by forgiving Him.

- *Pray.* Close your eyes and pray, placing your hand on your belly.
- *Inquire.* Ask, "Where did this get started in my life?"
- *First.* Focus on the first person or situation that comes to mind.

# TROUBLESHOOTING
## REMOVING FEAR

- **Pray.** Close your eyes and pray, placing your hand on your belly.
- **First.** You may see a situation, another person, or yourself.
- **Feel.** Allow yourself to feel the fear momentarily.
- **Forgive.** Receive forgiveness for taking in fear (see 1 John 4:18).

## Dealing with Lies

**Fact.** A lie may come in at the time of emotional wounding. In an attitude of prayer, ask the Lord to show you where it got started in your life. For example, *"My mother was always sick so I'm afraid I'll always be sick."*

- **Pray.** Close your eyes and pray, placing your hand on your belly.
- **First.** Allow the Lord to show you where the thought came in.
- **Feel.** Feel the feeling momentarily.
- **Forgive.** Forgive or receive forgiveness until you feel peace.
- **Fact.**
  - **Renounce.** Renounce the thought out loud.
  - **Welcome truth.** Ask God for the truth and welcome it into your heart.

## Filling Emotional Needs

Allow God to fill emotional needs that weren't met.

- **Pray.** Close your eyes and pray, placing your hand on your belly.
- **First.** Focus on the first person or situation that comes to mind.
- **Feel.** Feel the feeling momentarily.
- **Forgive.** Forgive or receive forgiveness until you feel peace.
- **Fact.**
  - **Renounce.** Renounce the thought (if any) out loud.
  - **Welcome truth.** If there was a lie, ask God for the truth and welcome it into your heart.
- **Fill.** If you have an emotional need that wasn't met (for example, love or approval) forgive those who should have met that need but didn't.
  - Release them into the hands of God until you no longer feel an inner demand concerning them.
  - When you have peace, welcome God to fill the need.

# ABOUT
# DENNIS AND DR. JEN CLARK

Dennis and Dr. Jen equip believers to heal themselves then facilitate healing to others. It is not counseling in the traditional sense, but a brand-new approach, teaching believers how to experience the peace of God in everyday life and how to deal quickly and completely with anything interrupting their peace. Some individuals may just want to receive quick healing for a few wounds and traumas, but many others have become committed to making peace a way of life, like the Clarks have learned to do.

They have spent years developing teaching materials based on spiritual revelation that have now been developed into targeted training modules that can be tailored for mature believers, new converts, Sunday school teachers, youth pastors, church discipleship programs, pastoral care, restoration, ministry teams, missionaries, and lay workers. The simple keys are easy enough for a mother or Sunday school worker to teach a three-year-old child, yet they are effective enough to heal the deepest hurts of adults quickly and completely. Advanced topics are also taught in other training seminars: dealing with the thought life, emotional health, willpower, addiction, deliverance, sexual issues, physical healing, and spiritual discernment.

Dennis and Dr. Jen are the authors of *Live Free: Discover the Keys to Living in God's Presence 24/7*, *Deep Relief Now: Simple Keys for Quickly Healing Your Longstanding Emotional Pain*, and *The Supernatural Power of Peace*. In addition, they have a series for children, *The Great God Quest*, which teaches the how-tos to children. They also have a series of eBooks: *Simple Keys to Heal Rejection*, *Simple Keys to Heal Loneliness*, and *Simple Keys for Self-Deliverance*. Dr. Jen is also the author of *Was Jesus a Capitalist?*

clark@forgive123.com

www.forgive123.com

"BECAUSE OF THE CLARKS' TEACHING, I CAN WALK IN SUPERNATURAL PEACE 24/7."
—SID ROTH, HOST, IT'S SUPERNATURAL!

THE
SUPER
NATURAL
POWER
OF
PEACE

DENNIS and DR. JEN CLARK

# GO BEYOND SELF HELP AND GET SPIRITUAL-HELP!

*Are you tired of dealing with the same problems over and over again? Do you feel emotionally burnt out?*

A times comes for everyone when theories and mental exercises just don't cut it, and you need something more to heal your pain. It's time to go beyond merely easing the hurt, and move towards complete, deep relief!

Dennis and Dr. Jen Clark share Biblical tools that will show you how to experience healing by living in the Spirit. This revolutionary new approach is a lifestyle adjustment that helps you break the continuous cycle of pain, and step into a new way of living—free, healed, and whole.

Because of Christ, you have received powerful tools capable of transforming the way you live. Deep Relief Now shows you how to put these tools into practice, break the pain cycle, and start living a healed lifestyle!

# OTHER TITLES BY
# DENNIS & DR. JEN CLARK

## Go Beyond Self-Help and get Spiritual Help!

A time comes for everyone when theories and mental exercises just don't cut it, and you need something more to heal your pain. It's time to go beyond merely easing the hurt, and move towards complete, deep relief!

## UNLOCK A LIFESTYLE OF FREEDOM IN GOD'S PRESENCE

None of us are exempt from getting hurt. The problem is what we do with pain. In *Live Free*, Dennis and Dr. Jen Clark offer a user-friendly guide to unlocking your lifestyle of freedom through intimacy with God.